# RIDING ON C

## A MEMOIR

"In voice, in person, on the radio, on the page, Cat Pleska has for years been one of my favorite writers. I carry the rhythms of her honeyed voice inside me. . . . Cat Pleska tells the story of her people with steady awareness of their hardships and foibles, their greatness of heart, and the smoking or alcohol that killed some of them, cut off in the midst of their stories while their inheritor, Cat, listens and faithfully records their voices for herself, for them, and for us. I could read this writer's words forever and still want more."

—Diana Hume George, author of *The Lonely Other: A Woman Watching America*

"The gifts of Cat Pleska's *Riding on Comets* are many: it is fresh, candid, gently humorous, tautly lyrical, and deeply moving. Cat Pleska writes masterfully and movingly about herself, her West Virginia home, and her colorful kin. But the greatest pleasure in reading *Riding on Comets* is that Pleska's prose refuses to stay on the page. Rather, it insists on being read aloud and filling the room with its rich rhythms, resonances, syntax, and family diction. Cat Pleska is a natural, graceful, spellbinding storyteller."

—Lisa Knopp, *What the River Carries: Encounters with the Mississippi, Missouri, and Platte*

"Cat Pleska's memoir of a childhood lived among the 'giants' of her West Virginia family is by turns humorous, touching, and achingly beautiful. This is a storyteller who knows how to piece together shards of a story into a brilliant mosaic of a life. A joy to read."

—Janice Gary is the author of *Short Leash: A Memoir of Dog Walking* and *Deliverance*, winner of two Silver 2014 Nautilus Awards and a 2014 Eric Hoffer Prize for Memoir

"*Riding on Comets* is not only a personal memoir, it is the story of a family embedded in West Virginia for many generations. . . . Cat Pleska's restrained but graceful prose allows us to witness four generations through the eyes of the author, first as a child and then through the years that followed as her people live, age, and die. The details Pleska offers have the immediacy of truths well told, with a resolute eye and spacious heart, neither shying away from family and personal dysfunction, nor sentimentalizing the bonds of fear and love that held her family together."

—Geoffrey Cameron Fuller is an author of the true crime *Pretty Little Killers* and the crime thriller *Full Bone Moon*

"Cat Pleska is a natural storyteller, a storied child. Growing up in West Virginia in the '50s and '60s, her life was steeped in family stories, and she was the one entrusted to retell them. Her own memories and experiences of small-town Appalachia deepen this candid and compelling coming-of-age memoir, and she captures our hearts in the process."

—Laura Treacy Bentley, author of *The Silver Tattoo* and *Lake Effect*

"This compelling memoir illumines a challenging childhood rooted in the town and countryside of West Virginia. It is an identifiably Appalachian life insightfully revealing a broader view of the region than stereotypes portray. It is, as well, pervaded with a razor-sharp honesty that brings heartfelt empathy to both the sweet and the wicked. I could not stop cheering for this spunky little girl who becomes a spirited and resourceful woman, a woman who never gives up on herself or those she loves."

—Marc Harshman, Poet Laureate of West Virginia and children's book author

"Image by image, each unquestionably whole and mysterious. . . . Those images—her grandmother offering a 'slice of apple from the edge of her knife,' the 'curing tobacco leaves hanging in bunches from the ceilings wooden beams' in a long abandoned house, or her 'Dad leaning over [her] mother's pristine, white enamel kitchen sink and throwing up blood'—tenderly sear themselves into both Cat's heart and the reader's. All these images reflect, compound, and resonate with one another until they carry us forward like a leaf swirling in the October wind."

—Chris Green, Director of the Loyal Jones Appalachian Center, Berea College

"Cat Pleska's memoir seamlessly moves through moments in time to discover that her story is her family's story of struggle and forgiveness against the backdrop of her native West Virginia mountains. Like stars that become constellations if we know how to look at them, this fine and engaging book shows us how to find and read the stories of our lives."

—Rob Merritt, author of *The Language of Longing*

"Sometimes comedic, sometimes heart wrenching . . . Cat Pleska writes with the graceful succinctness of a poet—whether she's describing a bike ride home 'pedaling fast against the dark' or just listening to the peepers 'calling out for someone to love them.'"

—Cheryl Ware, author of *Flea Circus Summer, Catty-Cornered, Venola in Love, Venola the Vegetarian,* and *Roberta Price Has Head Lice*

# RIDING
# ON
# COMETS

## CAT PLESKA

VANDALIA PRESS

MORGANTOWN 2015

First edition published 2015 by Vandalia Press

Printed in the United States of America

22 21 20 19 18 17 16 15 1 2 3 4 5 6 7 8 9

ISBN:

paper: 978-1-940425-51-1

epub: 978-1-940425-52-8

pdf: 978-1-940425-53-5

Cataloging-in-Publication Data is available at the Library in Congress

"The Time of Perfect Mud Pies" first appeared in the
*Anthology of Appalachian Writers*, 2013.
"Fall" and "Shelter" were recorded and aired on West Virginia
Public Radio, 2008.
"Riding on Comets" was recorded and aired on West Virginia
Public Radio, 2009.

Photo on front cover courtesy of the author.
Cover and book design by Than Saffel.

*This story is dedicated to my parents, Jean and Vernon, and my grandparents, Opal and Warren.*

# CONTENTS

STRENGTH . . .

# ACKNOWLEDGMENTS

I AM ONE LUCKY CAT. I have my family to thank: my parents, who urged me to tell their stories, and my grandparents who told me wonderful stories. To aunts, uncles, and cousins, thanks for your indulgence with my perception of events.

Many thanks to all the writing teachers I worked with over the years. Early supporters: Jean Anaporte and Sandra Marshburn. My mentors from Goucher: Lisa Knopp, Kevin Kerrane, Tom French, and especially Diana Hume George, mentor and dear friend. A special thanks to my program director, Patsy Sims. To my Goucher classmates: Go Gophers!

Heartfelt thanks to friend Denise Long, my pal since we were both seven. My dear friend Debra Juliana Eichenberger, who always believed in me. To supporting and loving friends over the years, many thanks: Pam Folden, Lee Maynard, Shari Heywood, Keith Davis, Carla McClure, Pat McClure, Phyllis Wilson Moore, Ann Pancake, Eddy Pendarvis, Christine Roth, Christina Peraino, Patty Cole, Linda Riffe, Meredith Sue Willis, and Pops Walker.

Thanks to my friends and fellow writers: Sheila McEntee; Fran Simone; Belinda Anderson; Laura Treacy Bentley; Marie Manilla; Jeanette Eberhardy; Jan Gary; InSuk Granholm;

Cynthia Toomey; Sunday at 2 writers group; and my spiritual writing partners, Karyn Cantees Stagg and Michelle Bowers.

To my writing students over the years: many thanks to you. (You know who you are!) What I learned from each of you helped me become a better writer, a better person.

Thanks to my acquisitions editor at West Virginia University Press, Abby Freeland.

And last, but most certainly not least, I want to acknowledge my beautiful daughter, Katie Pleska, whose patience is phenomenal and also my steady-as-a-rock husband, Dan. Love you both.

# AUTHOR'S NOTES

I HAVE BEEN REMEMBERING FOR twenty years, thinking about this book. The memories recorded here are mine, however imperfect they might be, but all as true as I can recall. They are also memories of family and friends, some blended, some in contrast. Perception is a fascinating conundrum, and I respect different memories, as well as my own. The dialogue, though re-created, is written to feel authentic. As a child of storytellers, many words from the past are like learned speaking parts of a play.

Finally, my effort was always to write about myself and others with a sense of dignity and respect. I may have missed my marks, but I tried hard to do my best.

Some people's names and details have been purposely left out or altered to protect privacy.

# THE TIME OF PERFECT MUD PIES

WHEN IT WAS THE TIME of perfect mud pies, the rain had fallen steadily throughout the hot summer day. I remember standing in the middle of the dirt road in front of my grandparents' house when I was five, watching the mist writhe around the hills. My gaze fell to the bounty below me. Rain had created puddle after puddle, ranging in depth from ankle deep to barely covering my toes.

And lucky me: I detected a trapped rainbow on the puddles' surface. My grandfather and uncles spread used motor oil on the road to calm the dust, but little did they know it would create a colorful display. Still, motor oil helped turn the mud a deep, ashy brown. It was an exotic ingredient. My small hands scooped mud that squished and burbled through my fingers: not too much grit, not too much clay, and pebble free.

I molded the thick mud patties, then lined them around one particularly deep hole, probably eight or ten patties. After admiring my handiwork for a moment, I snatched one up and took a bite. Mud flowed into my mouth leaving grit on my teeth and tongue. At first, it tasted—earthy, but then bitter and metallic.

I sucked on the grit, pondering what to do. I looked up to see the surrounding land on either side of my little spot in the road.

Everything was weighted with rain. I smelled the sharp green of grass and wildflowers. From where I stood, I glimpsed the garden with its reaching bean vines, drooping corn tassels. To the side of the garden, my grandparents' lone cow grazed, and in lifting my head higher, beyond rolled hill after hill of trees.

My tongue searched my mouth for more grit. The cold, molten brownness mixed with the saliva that came forth to greet the mud, and then I swallowed. I instantly wanted milk from my grandmother's refrigerator. I spit, but the grit remained.

The patty in my hand, with a small bite from its side, sat solid and heavy. With my fingertip, I smoothed the place where I had bitten, then put it back among the others.

I studied the possibilities for my mud pies. I had hoped to sell them. They were so pretty, and surely they must have a hamburger or chocolate flavor. After that taste-testing, however, I thought . . . perhaps not. I squatted and pushed them one by one back in the mud hole. On another day to create, perhaps I would make something useful, a mud thing that would last. I would think about it.

I looked toward my grandparents' house. If I wanted to play on my grandmother's clean porch, I'd have to wash the mud from my hands and face. I'd have to slip past my grandmother, forever cleaning, but most often at the stove cooking.

Then I noted my dirty clothes. It was one thing to wash the grit from my face and hands, but it was another to have muddied my clothes so thoroughly. She would not be pleased.

When I entered the house, my grandmother was leaning against the sink peeling potatoes. She was dressed in red capris and a loose, white blouse, her dark hair wrapped in a kerchief. I had to go through the kitchen to get to the bathroom. *Ah, her back is turned*, I thought. But so young, I had not learned to sneak on a creaky wooden floor. Immediately, she spotted me tiptoeing behind the table.

"Where have you been?"

I froze then turned to see her eyeing me up and down. Throwing down her knife, she came to me and put a firm hand on my back and marched me into the bathroom.

As she scrubbed my face vigorously with a warm, wet cloth, she paused. "Let me see your teeth." I bared them in a grin. "Your mother's going to kill me." She resumed her scrubbing this time right on my teeth. Finally, she dabbed at the mud spots on my shorts and top, clucking, clucking. "Stay right there." She straightened, throwing the cloth in the sink, and left the bathroom to return with clean clothes. She stripped me and dressed me in a fresh blouse and shorts. She nodded and told me to scoot and to stay clean until supper. "I'll have to tell your mommy," she threatened as I fled to the front porch.

My transgression, however, was forgotten by suppertime, with no mention of my muddied state to my parents, who arrived shortly before my grandmother placed dinner on the table. They would take me home later that night, as I had school the next day. We ate real hamburgers, on soft white bread, with plenty of mayonnaise and pepper. Fried potatoes and just-from-the-garden green beans—most disappeared quickly.

As soon as I finished eating, I raced out the back door. The fog had descended, now lying at the base of the hills. Humidity smothered. As I stood, belly full, relieved I had escaped punishment, I studied the mist, listening to the tree frogs, peepers as we called them. I heard chairs scrape the floor as my family left the table, exiting the kitchen, heading toward the front porch.

Inside the house, the air moved thanks to fans clutched in the open windows. The screens on the front and back doors kept flies out and allowed a good breeze as if they were the house's lungs.

An aunt and uncle had joined us at the dinner table, and now they gathered again, claiming first one chair, then another. I waited on my grandmother, always late after securing leftover food in the refrigerator.

She chose a green metal lawn chair, and as soon as she sat, I immediately sought the comfort of her lap. She balanced me while holding a cup of coffee in one hand and a cigarette in the other. I smelled the tang of tobacco. As the evening deepened, heat lightning flashed off to the west, flipping up over the hills. I liked nightfall, the deep and comforting inkiness, when whole bodies disappeared in the dark. I rested my head against her chest and listened to the *tha thump tha thump* of her heart. I watched the red glow at the end of everyone's cigarettes lighten and darken as they inhaled.

No one spoke at first. Thoughts must gather. Night sounds must register. The darkness would allow the voices to come forth in their own time.

My aunt moved back inside to turn on the living room lamp and then returned. A soft shaft of light from the window fell on the knot of us. A few words came with great silences in between. Grunts of agreement. Coffee sips. Finally, conversation picked up speed and intensity. My eyes adjusted to the dark, and I saw frowns creep over the rims of coffee cups or cigarette smoke blown from noses. Sometimes, the listeners would jostle cups, wiping tears from their eyes, laughing, catching their breath after a tall tale.

"I heard Phyllis died," my mother said. "It was her liver. I remember when we worked together at the dime store. Mr. Fitzpatrick, the manager, would holler at me, 'Miz Akens! Miz Akens! We need more Kotex out on the counter!' He'd just do that to bug me. He couldn't say Atkins right."

"Yes, I remember," my grandmother nodded, chuckling. I shifted my weight on her lap. "It seems to me people ain't supposed to die young. But you never know . . ." Her body stilled. "I'm worried about Jean. She don't seem right lately." My grandmother's voice rumbled through my ears, reverberated in my chest, and lodged so deeply in my psyche that I thought this was the way everyone in the world must sound.

I heard a *gallump* as she swallowed her coffee. In the dim light, I peered at my mother, whose name is also Jean. My grandmother was speaking of my Aunt Jean who occasionally took me to town in her big, Pepto-Bismol pink Ford. Always there'd be candy in bags on the front seat. She had to eat it once in a while, she'd told me. Something about "sugar," but she always let me have pieces of her candy.

For a while, no one said anything. Stilled bodies began to shift again. Then, like a rainstorm, I knew a story was coming. My grandmother launched into her tale about when I almost died.

"Well, it was the middle of winter," my grandmother began. "Cathy was sick." She pointed to me with her cigarette. "No kids ever get the croup in the summer. Anyhow, she was about a year old or so. Jean and Vernon was staying up in the cellar house then. But Vernon and Warren was at work, and Cathy started turning blue." She paused, took a drag from her cigarette. She looked at me, and in the dim light I imagined her warm brown eyes. She talked sometimes with a cigarette in her mouth, and I watched its glowing red end near my face. I snuggled deeper into her chest.

"She had membrane croup. That's what they called it then. She was choking and a-burning up with fever. Her mommy like to have went nuts. It started snowing that morning after Vernon and Warren left and just kept piling up. The phone lines was still working, and we called the doctor. He said he'd not try to make it up the holler because the snow was so deep, and most likely she'd be dead before he got here. He'd try to make it the morning." I watched as smoke rolled out of her nose. She picked a bit of tobacco from her tongue.

"Well, I hung up that phone, and I says to her mommy, 'Give me that baby. I'll open her up.' I cut up a whole bunch of onions and fried them up in a skillet. When they got tender, I put them on layers of cheesecloth and stripped Cathy down to her diaper. I took her in the TV room and turned her feet toward the fire and molded them onions onto her chest. It wasn't long, and she was breathing good." My grandmother chuckled and my body vibrated.

Snorts came from around the porch. "It's a shame," my mom said, "the way doctors don't care no more. Why, a body could die because the doctor didn't tell her she wasn't supposed to eat licorice every day. Does terrible things to the liver."

****

On the evening of the day of perfect mud pies, I remained on the porch listening to the women. But on some hot evenings I'd join the men, who usually went back to the kitchen or stayed there to start with to be near the cold beer. My grandfather, at the end of the oak table, allowed me to salt his beer, both of us watching the foam rise, or I'd roll his cigarettes with his cigarette-rolling machine. His chuckles at the simple things I did or said began deep in his big belly, then grumbled up into harrumphing lungs. Finally, he'd laugh-cough. He wore tan or green work shirts and pants and steel-toed boots. He only wore a suit to a funeral or when he and my grandmother went to talk to Jack Wilson at the bank to get a loan for a new truck. His hair was grey-flecked blond and his eyes a transparent blue.

Other men at my grandfather's table—maybe my dad and a few uncles—needed salt in their beers, too, so my presence was necessary. They'd talk about the day's work, hunting or fishing, or about a car that needed a new engine.

"Dad, the company still got you welding collars on live gas lines? Don't think I'd wanna try a weld that can blow you to kingdom come if it don't take right."

My grandfather inhaled on his cigarette. Smoke tumbled out haphazardly as he talked. "Still gotta hang upside down in a bell hole to weld those collars on." My grandfather laughed, went into a coughing fit, then flipped cigarette ashes into a glass dish. "You gotta ease the oxygen in or it gets hot too fast. Get'er to white-hot fast, and that gas line'll blow. Spit on the weld. That'll tell you if it's the right temperature."

My grandfather was an expert welder, I'd heard my father say. He was a fine shot with the rifle and shotgun, though my dad was the better fisherman. They hunted often and told tales of deer with big racks or of the elusive and cunning brown trout. Sometimes, my grandfather or my father would launch into the story of a night on Cheat Mountain.

I have remembered their words, their inflections, the rhythms of body and voice.

****

Then, as ever on these hot summer nights, I'd fall asleep. Whether it was at my grandparents' or in my own home, someone would carry me to a big bed with sweet-smelling, sun-dried sheets. As if from a distance, I'd hear my mother's soft voice telling me to put my little head down on the chop block and dream sweet dreams. She'd tuck a lock of hair behind my ear, then tiptoe out.

I slept the deep sleep of a storied child, not knowing what I'd face as I grew.

I have struggled to keep their stories in the shape in which they formed them. I try to pat them just so, make them taste gritty and sharp, misty and magical. These people, and the land, began the shaping of me until I could continue on my own.

IMAGES . . .

# CHAPTER 1

# NO SALT

A LATE AUTUMN SUN SLANTED through the window over the kitchen sink. White curtains, with a cheerful, yellow rickrack trim, fluttered with the breeze. My mother had a knack for making things pretty even though she had next to nothing. She scrubbed the red vinyl countertop, straightened the silverware drawer, wiped the stove, rearranged the dish towels, opened and shut empty cabinet doors.

*Salt. If I only had a bit of salt, the potatoes boiling on the stove would sure taste better. And butter. Her kingdom and her horse for butter,* she thought.

I was there, but I couldn't have known about any of this at the time: the loneliness, the hungry belly, the fear that crept in past her bravado as she sang around the kitchen, keeping busy. I was nine months in the womb. When she sang, maybe I heard the gentle tones to lull me to sleep. If I was jolted as she bumped against the counter, I may have rolled over in protest.

My father had left her alone with no food, no money, no car, only a phone. She hummed against her fears, as if they held at bay the stomach growls, the disbelief he'd been gone for days, and the fact she had no idea where he was, or if he was coming back. She'd called his mother to ask if she'd seen him, and my grandmother, from a generation of women who protected the men, said she had not seen her son. My mother learned much later he was passed out on his mother's couch at the time.

My dad must have seemed to my mom like an answer to her dreams. He was Robert Mitchum handsome, funny, assured. He looked incredibly fit in his Army uniform, and worldly, having just returned from the Korean War. By her own admission, she was as green as grass when she married him. I was to be a honeymoon baby. They married on a mild January day and rented a small house, secluded up on College Hill in Saint Albans. He was a good, reliable employee for the gas company, except when he missed work once in a while when he was drinking. My mother said she was never sure when he'd be gone for a few days, or if he was still alive. She had no way to go around to the beer joints and look for him.

So I rolled over in her belly and slept the sleep of the innocent, deep and peaceful. He came home after three weeks. My mother never told me what she said to him when he finally returned. My experience from watching them over the years tells me she probably didn't say much. With a shortened education and no belief in herself she could do better, "What choice did I have?" she'd ask me each time she told me this story. I knew she didn't expect an answer from me.

One thing she made sure I knew: "It is his fault he is like this. It is not my fault nor is it yours."

It was the only defense she had.

It would be years before I learned the reason for my father's drinking.

# CHAPTER 2

# TRICK OR TREAT

MY MOTHER PACED MY GRANDPARENTS' small kitchen. It was 7:00 p.m., October 31, 1953. She stopped occasionally and rubbed her belly when another contraction hit. My father was in the bathroom, shaving. He'd come in earlier from squirrel hunting, and when my mother told him she was going into labor, he disappeared into the bathroom to clean up. Nervous, she continued to pace, waiting. An hour later, they were on their way.

When they got to Thomas Memorial Hospital, a county away, Mom was wheeled into a room and examined by Dr. Soulsby, who said, "This baby isn't coming today. This is false labor. I'm sending you home." But her contractions remained strong, so he decided it was best to keep her overnight. It was getting late, and he'd release her in the morning. He was wrong. I was born fifteen minutes before midnight on Halloween.

Mom would tease me about my birth: "I'm pretty sure you were born with your shoes on." Apparently, I was a painful process. When I was old enough to reply, I teased back, "How would you know? They knocked mothers out back then. You slept through the whole thing."

She'd snort, "I'm just tellin' ya."

# CHAPTER 3

# A TONE

AT THE FOOT OF A white metal bed, I planted my bare toes on the lowest rung, stretched up, and strained to see my great-grandmother, Ida Mae. Peeking over my hands that grasped the top rail, I saw a puff of beige-pink face sunk deep into a pillow. Her face reminded me of those tiny mushrooms I'd seen on the forest floor. Her small head was barely covered with wisps of hair. Her eyes remained closed, and her lips were pursed, as if she were thinking. Fingers, the color of earthworms that float on the sidewalk after a hard rain, curled under her chin. Her body was a skinny bump under the white coverlet; she looked no taller than me. I was four.

"What's wrong with her?" I asked.

"She's dying."

I had no idea what that meant, but I glanced up and watched the faces of my mother, a couple of aunts, my grandmother. They frowned, hovered around the bed, restless. Occasionally, one reached out a hand and placed it on Ida's forehead, as if testing for fever.

The room was illuminated through one window—washing a brilliant light over everything—but especially Ida Mae as she lay among white bed linens. I watched her out of the corner of my eye and saw a faint gold glow hugging closely to her body.

Turning my head back to her, it would disappear. Over and over I turned my head, seeking the gold band. There, gone, there, gone. Then it vanished from my vision at any angle, and only the bright, blue-white light from the window washed over her.

I was looking fully at her when, suddenly, her chest rose as she inhaled deeply. Her mouth fell open and something dark appeared at the corners, and that's when I noticed she had no teeth. Quickly, Mom grabbed me under the arms and carried me out of the room and into the next. "Stay here," she told me. She shut the door. I studied the grain pattern in the door, reaching out, tracing it with my finger. I waited.

****

Much later, after the funeral, when we got back to my grandparents' house, my grandmother and my mom opened Ida's bedroom door. They plucked the pillow off the bed then slipped off the pillowcase. With a large pair of scissors, my grandmother ripped open the pillow and reached inside. She pulled out a flattened, round mass of feathers. "It's a feather crown," Mommaw said, and handed it to Mom. "Ida's in heaven," they said.

After they left the room, I picked up the rosette of feathers and marveled at how it was so tightly woven I could not pluck out a single feather. How is this thing made? Who had woven it and stuffed it in Ida Mae's pillow? Where is heaven? What is it like? I put the rosette back on the bed and left the bedroom.

# CHAPTER 4

# GIVE ME MY HAT

He came around the corner so fast that I froze in my spot on the sidewalk in fear. I hadn't thought he was so close to me. He saw me then and raised his cane to strike me, but I turned and ran. I didn't stop until I reached the creek. I looked behind me. He was standing at the back door of my grandparents' house, facing it, just staring. He reached up with a hand and smoothed his white beard. Then he opened the screen door and slowly stepped inside the house.

It was not the first time I'd teased my great-grandfather, George, to chase me. I never said anything to him, but I would run up to him, wait until he raised his cane. Then I ran. I knew he was too old to catch me, but that time he'd surprised me with how fast he had moved.

My dad had told me his grandfather used to teach in one-room schoolhouses in Lincoln and Putnam Counties. He traveled on a horse and spent the week staying in people's homes while he taught at a nearby school. He was a hard teacher, my dad said, one you didn't mess with.

Now his mind was gone, Mommaw had told me. He was forgetful, didn't remember who people were. My great-grandmother Ida had been the same way. George and Ida fought sometimes, Mommaw told me. One time, she came into their bedroom to hear the two of them arguing over his hat. Ida lay "buck naked," Mommaw said, in the bed, save for George's hat. George wanted his hat back, and she wouldn't give it to him. He was mad at her and yelled. "They were like children," Mommaw said.

Ida made quilts, and one she had made for my dad was now on my bed in my house. It was mostly pink fabrics, a color I didn't like, but it was Ida's, Mom told me. And so there it was on my bed, as if that made sense. Ida loved my dad, Mom said. Dad said he used to run up to Ida and George's house, just a little ways up the road, when he was little. He'd hide in the barn's hayloft and read the Bible. Dad said he could read it and understand what it said when he was only five.

When it was dinnertime, Ida would call Dad in to eat. The house smelled of biscuits; mashed potatoes, with a quarter stick of butter melting on top; meat and gravy; fresh green beans; and fried green tomatoes. George would say the blessing that this food would nourish their bodies and souls so they might serve the Lord, amen.

George wanted my dad to go to college, become a teacher. He'd pay for it, he said. But my dad didn't do that. He dropped out of school just after the tenth grade to go work in the navy shipyards in Baltimore, Maryland, when he was sixteen. Dad had been double-promoted twice, and if George was disappointed in Dad, no one ever said.

When Ida died, an event I missed because Mom had lifted me out of the room, a framed photo fell off the wall just as Ida stopped breathing. Its string was unbroken, the nail unbent, but the picture fell from the wall as if yanked. It was a photo of one of Ida's grandchildren. Mom told me about it many times.

One day, Mommaw missed George from the house and went looking for him. He came home on his own, covered with purple juice. He had eaten poisonous poke berries. He fell ill and they took him to the hospital, but it was too late to save him.

# CHAPTER 5

# BIG EARL'S

THREE WET, PINK NOSES SNUFFLED along a fence board. Six pink ears bobbed as chubby bodies jiggled in place, eager for their food to splash in the trough in front of them. I stepped onto the bottom fence board and grabbed the top rail to peer into the pigpen, waiting for Poppaw to dump the beige-colored slop. The pigs squealed as he emptied his bucket, then plunged their slimy snouts into the trough, snarfling and snuffling as they sucked up the food. Behind them, thousands of cloven hoofprints marked the mud. Beyond was a small crib where the pigs slept.

*That is strange,* I was thinking. *Wynken didn't have a large block blotch on his side when I last saw him before Thanksgiving last year. Nod seemed awful small, now that I was looking at him. Wasn't he the biggest? How did he shrink? Blynken was smaller, too, and I was pretty sure he had a notch in his ear.*

A little earlier, as we'd left the kitchen to feed Wynken, Blynken, and Nod, Mommaw said it was going to be one of those scorching June days. It was early morning, but already the dew had dried, the sky was clear, and the sun was hot on our shoulders. I had been staying with Mommaw and Poppaw for a few weeks before I began first grade in September. I loved staying with them.

I let go of the top rail and reached toward what I thought was Nod.

"Now, don't you touch them, Punkin Head," Poppaw said. "Don't ever reach your hand through the fence. They can be mean. Hurt chuh." Poppaw waved me back with his big hand. I stepped off the fence board and moved back to watch the pigs gobble up the slop. My oats had looked a lot better that morning as I had watched Mommaw dab on sweet cream butter and then pour on cold milk, globby with fat.

As Poppaw and I walked down the slope back to the house, he swung the empty slop bucket with one hand and ruffled my hair with the other. He'd often steer me with his hand on my head so I wouldn't wander off and get into trouble, he said. Other times, I held onto one of his fingers that was so big it fit into my whole hand.

Poppaw set the bucket down on the sidewalk, and we found the kitchen empty when we stepped into it. It still smelled wonderful from last night's fried chicken. "Pet!" Poppaw hollered. He moved over to the table to pick up his pack of Camels and lit one, letting the smoke roll out into the room. "Pet!" he yelled louder. "Your Mommaw musta went up the holler, Stinker." That was the other name Poppaw called me. It was either Punkin Head or Stinker. "How 'bout me and you go on over ta Big Earl's?"

I nodded, fine with following Poppaw anywhere.

We went out and around to the side of the house to get into his black pickup. He swung me up on the seat then passed around the front of the truck and climbed in behind the steering wheel. I moved over toward him, standing on the seat to put my arm around the back of his thick neck. I was short, but still

I had to lean over a little to keep my head from bumping the truck's ceiling. From my position, I could see the road ahead of us just fine. He shifted the truck into reverse and backed down the short driveway to the dirt lane leading down to the hard road.

As we rumbled down Route 60, I noticed each wide seam in the paved highway jarred the truck and made me feel as if my teeth rattled. I loved that the wind blowing into the cab lifted the skirt of my sky-blue dress.

I knew we were headed toward "Mandyville," as everyone called Amandaville, a little town next to Saint Albans, where my Mommaw went shopping for groceries. I knew about Big Earl, the bootlegger who lived in Mandyville, because Poppaw visited there a lot. I had no idea what a bootlegger was. I only knew Mommaw drove Poppaw there on Sundays. He'd come home with a bottle in a brown paper bag, the top of the bag scrunched around the neck with only the tip showing. He'd sit at the end of the kitchen table and sip out of it for the rest of the day, then go to bed and cuss in his sleep. I learned all my bad words from him, I heard my Mom say. I knew she wasn't too happy about it.

But I was excited. This was the first time Poppaw ever said he'd take me to Big Earl's.

We didn't pass any cars, and I twisted in the seat to look back, but no cars followed us either. I turned around and watched his hands on the steering wheel. Big as canned hams, my Mom said. He had one elbow propped in his open window.

He slowed the truck and turned onto a dirt road. Houses on both sides were small and white, with lots of dust settled in the dips of the siding. I didn't see any kids playing, but toys were spread everywhere: tricycles, wagons, dolls with no clothes. Cars sat up on blocks, and most of the yards had no grass. I saw a tire swing hanging from the limb of a tree that didn't have any leaves. The swing looked fun. No one was around except a brown dog curled up in the dirt.

Poppaw stopped the truck in front of a little white house at the end of the street, its paint peeling and a black screen door half hanging off its hinges. White chickens scratched the dirt under a big old tree. A small dust devil swirled from the yard to the street, a sure sign of rain, Mommaw always said. I loved dust devils. I wanted to run into one. I was sure it would lift me up in the air, and I'd float with the dirt and leaves, but she said it might be dangerous, and I wasn't to run inside the things. "Might suck you up and set you down in the creek," she said.

The truck stopped, and Poppaw turned to look at me as he turned off the motor: "You stay here, Stinker. I'll be back in a minute." He slid out of the truck, hitched up his beige work pants, and stepped onto the porch, which gave with his weight. He swung open the screen door and disappeared into the black inside.

I stood and stared ahead where Poppaw had gone. I watched the white chickens peck the ground, but after a while, I began to look around. I heard shouting to my right—men's voices. A little way from where our truck was parked was a wooden fence. The voices were coming from behind. Suddenly, a few bird feathers floated up and then slowly drifted down and back out of sight. I'd seen those kinds of feathers before. They were on a black velvet hat I'd found in Mommaw's back closet. These feathers fascinated me because, black as they were, it was a trick. When I took the hat to the window to look at the feathers in a brighter light, they shimmered with the colors of the rainbow.

I walked along the seat and rested my hands on the door to look out the open window. A gap in the fence where boards had fallen over framed a view of a dirt yard behind. I couldn't see much but bits and pieces of men and birds—the birds were chickens, but not like the white ones in the yard with red combs. These were roosters. I saw two men, first one, then the other as they moved around. Each was holding a rooster, their big claws stretching out in front. I heard a person shout, "Pit!" and the men let go of their roosters. The birds plopped on the ground and began kicking one another. Then they started rolling over and over together, stirring up dust. Then they rolled out of my sight.

Suddenly, a man's black face appeared at the gap in the board. He moved his head so mostly one eye looked at me. He turned his head a little, and I saw his teeth, or what ones he had. I could see gum, too, and the teeth he did have were brown and white. His face disappeared, and a couple fingers snaked through the gap. He wiggled them, then put his eye back to the hole. He seemed to be saying something, but I couldn't hear with the voices yelling behind him and the roosters squawking. *Funny man*, I thought. *What was he saying?* I leaned a little farther out the window.

His lips came into the hole and he pursed them, like he was kissing at me. I leaned a little further. *Was he talking to me?*

A screen door banging caught my attention, and I looked over to see Poppaw coming off the porch and toward the truck. I glanced back at the fence, but the man was gone. Again I watched the roosters fighting. I worried about them hurting one another.

"Ready to go home, Stinker?" Poppaw said as he swung himself up into the truck. I plopped down onto the seat.

"Yeah, Poppaw."

He started the motor. He backed up the truck, and we were headed down the street and to the hard road. Between us on the seat was a bottle in a brown paper bag. I couldn't get as close to Poppaw with the bottle tight against his leg. Out the windshield, I watched the clear sky. Once in a while we'd pass a tree, its top leaning over like it was looking in the truck at us. I turned my head and looked out the side window, where I saw treetops flashing by in a blur. Then I saw the top half of another dust devil. It had picked up leaves and little bits of paper. It swirled at the side of the road.

*What would it be like to step into that dust devil*, I thought. *To float above the trees. Maybe no one could see me because my dress was the same color as the sky. I'd just float and float.*

I looked over at Poppaw. He drew deeply on a cigarette, and the smoke rolled out the open window. As we bumped over the cracks in the hard road, I thought: *I want Poppaw to stop the truck. I want to run into the devil and float up and back to Mandyville. I want it to set me down on the other side of the fence.*

# CHAPTER 6

# A BRUSH WITH THE LAW

THE SUN HAD NOT YET warmed the day when my friend Eddie and I placed our Bobbsey Twins sand pails side by side at the foot of a big hill. He started digging in the dirt with his shovel, lifting off big pieces of grass and setting them to the side. I was five, a year younger than Eddie, and I wanted to do everything he did. So I started digging, too. It was hard at first, lifting out big clods of black soil, but then the digging got easier. The black dirt smelled strong, and I dug up earthworms that I accidentally cut in two with my shovel. But I piled them on my growing dirt mound and thought each half would find the other half, and maybe they'd go back together.

We were squatting, digging, when I suddenly felt my foot sting. Earlier, I had stepped on an open, metal Band-Aid box, and the sharp pain had brought tears. I had looked at my foot and saw blood running onto the ground from a big cut. It began to throb, so I ground it into the cool sand in our sandbox. That stopped the bleeding, eased the pain. That's when Eddie showed up with his digging plan. We'd dig in the bottom of the big hill at the back of our apartment building. Why, I didn't really know, but Eddie wanted to do it, and I was okay with that.

I don't know how long we dug, but our piles of dirt were built up pretty good. Then Eddie decided he was hungry and wanted to go to his apartment, down the hall from mine. So we put our shovels in our pails—his was blue and mine was red— and decided to come back later to keep digging.

I climbed the steps to the second floor at the back of the apartment building and walked down the long, dark hallway to the front of the building to my apartment. As I got closer, I saw a policeman talking to Mom, who was standing in the open doorway. He looked down at me as I got closer. He said, "That's her?" Mom nodded and he laughed and said, "Well, I have to check these things out. I guess you should tell her not to do that anymore." They continued to talk, but I slipped past them into the living room.

The living room was also my bedroom because the apartment had only one bedroom, and it belonged to my parents. I didn't mind sleeping on the couch. The brand new television sat across from the couch, and I easily watched *Steamboat Bob*, *Howdy Doody*, or cartoons.

I stood listening to the policeman and Mom talk, and I began to worry. I'd earlier peeled the numbers off everyone's mailboxes that were fixed on the apartment building's wall. The numbers were shiny gold, and they came off so easily. When they were all off and lying in a pile in my hand, I realized perhaps I shouldn't have done that. I tried to put them back, but I had no idea what number went with which box, and I wasn't too sure of my numbers yet, anyway. Now, here was a policeman, probably to take me to jail.

The policeman left. Mom asked what I'd been doing that morning.

I told her I'd been playing in the sandbox and helping Eddie dig.

"Dig what?" she wanted to know.

"The big hill out back."

"You mean the flood wall?"

"What's a flood wall?" I asked.

Mom laughed. "Well, it's a big hill of dirt that keeps the river from flooding over into the yard when it rains too much." She left then to go into the kitchen to make lunch. She didn't say anything else, so I thought I shouldn't say anything about the numbers . . . just yet.

Later in the day, when Dad got home, I listened as Mom told him what had happened.

"You mean a grown woman called the police on Cat and Eddie for digging at the base of the flood wall?" He shook his head and laughed. "We were in real danger because the base of that wall must be seventy-five feet thick, at least."

"Well, you know she doesn't like kids. She didn't want any of us with children moving in these apartments. She's batty as they come."

They both turned to look at me. I grinned. I was glad no one knew about the numbers on the mailboxes.

By bedtime the pain in my foot was back, stronger than before. I showed Mom, who lifted me up to the edge of the bathtub and ran cold water over the cut, trying to flush out the firmly packed sand. She put cream on the gash and wrapped it in gauze. I limped for a week, making my playmates want a gash too. I told them how to do it, but none of them tried.

# CHAPTER 7

# IN MOMMAW'S KITCHEN

IN MOMMAW'S KITCHEN, ON A cold, grey day, I ate apple cinnamon cookies and watched her have her hair cut by her second cousin, Aggie. Or maybe she was a third cousin. I don't think anyone knew for sure. We sat at my grandparents' oak table. The glass in the windows over the sink was covered with sweat, making the outside look wavy.

Aggie snatched at a tangle in Mommaw's hair.

"Ouch."

"Sorry," Aggie said.

I slipped over near them and lifted the lid of a pink ceramic pig cookie jar, setting it on the table. If the jar remained uncovered, it'd be easier to pluck out a cookie or two.

"Now, that's enough of them cookies. You're gonna get the bellyache," Mommaw said and frowned at me. I scuttled around the table, moving from chair to chair until I got back to where I had started. Sitting down, I swung my feet, which were several inches off the floor, clapping the heels of my shoes. I munched on my cookies. She pointed to the coffee pot on the stove.

"Get yourself more coffee there, Aggie. I could probably take another cup," she said as she pulled a hair off her blouse that had slipped past the towel draped around her shoulders.

"Uh huh, uh huh," Aggie said then laid the comb and scissors down and went over to the stove. As she poured the black, strong coffee, Mommaw said, "Did I tell you the assessor was here the other day?"

"No," Aggie said.

"Yeah, he was. He was sitting right there." She pointed to the chair sitting along one side of the table. I stared at the chair a while with her. Aggie returned to combing Mommaw's hair.

"Asked me a buncha questions. I remember Warren talked to one of them afore, not long after we was married. Anyhow, he was at work when this little feller showed up. I said, 'What do you want to know all that stuff for?' He said he was supposed to ask so they knowed how many cows and hogs we had. New buildings. It was for taxes. But he was just wanting to know how it was. I gave him coffee. He set a spell."

"Uh huh, uh huh," Aggie said.

"I told him there ain't much ever goes on around here, you know? Lord, special in the winter. Look at them trees. All bare. Ain't no green to be had," she continued.

"I'll swan," Aggie said. I noticed Aggie said "I'll swan" a lot. Mom said that was old folks' way of saying "I swear." I supposed so. I'd finished my two cookies. I plotted how to get more.

"He said he was working his way to most houses. It'd been a while, he said, since that'd been done. Is the coffee boiling again? Just want it to simble. Cathy, go check it will you, hon?"

I figured if I went around to do that, I might casual-like grab another cookie or two.

"For the assessor's office you say?" That was Aggie asking.

"Yeah. They'll raise our taxes no doubt. He was nice. His

hair was all slicked back, and he had on a black suit and tie."
She didn't seem to notice I'd taken two more cookies before I
sat back down after turning the flame down under the coffee.

"Uh huh," Aggie said.

"He asked me what Warren did for a living. I told him he
was at the gas company now twenty-some year. Doing the same
thing as always, welding pipe. He said maybe his dad worked
with Warren. He'd been at the gas company ten year."

"That so?" Aggie asked.

"Yeah," Mommaw chuckled. "You know what? He asked me
what I did. He said women was going out and getting jobs now.
I don't know how. How they gonna do that and keep a house
and kids? He said *he* didn't know."

She and Aggie laughed.

"He wanted to know how long we'd lived here. I had to think
back. Pop built this house in '30, maybe '28. The big house was
there before it blew up from a gas line leak."

"Uh huh, uh huh," Aggie said.

"You know I never did know what happened to that family. They's a daughter I think lives down on Route 60. I got a
picture around here somewhere. They's standing there all bandaged up. Warren's dad later bought this property, and my dad
built this house for us."

"I'll swan," Aggie said.

I'd seen the photo of that family. Whenever I visited my
grandparents, I plundered through the dresser drawers looking for photos. I imagined what happened to them. Maybe
the mom, who had her head wrapped in bandages, became
the mummy's wife in the movies. One boy, about my age had
his hands bandaged. He was holding a little dog. Maybe he

wandered all over the country begging for biscuits for his little doggy, seeing as how he couldn't work with his hands.

While Mommaw was busy telling a story, I snuck around and got two more cookies.

"Anyway, I guess it was all right to tell him all that. He said it didn't sound too dull around here to him. I told him he ought to live here, and he would know just how it was."

Aggie picked up the scissors again and started trimming more hair, which fell on the floor, Mommaw's shoulders and on the table some.

"Course, there was the other day when them boys of mine showed themselves. You hear about that?"

"No," Aggie said.

"Drunk, ever one of them. Warren, too. They decided to race their cars up the side of the hill over there." She pointed out the window over the sink. All I saw were wavy bare trees.

"I'd gone to the cellar to get a jar of sauerkraut; they decided they'd race to see who would get to the top of the hill first. Lord, they liked to have scared me to death. You never heard such noise, smoke rolling out from under the tires, just a-tearing them cars up. Me screaming the whole time to stop."

"I'll swan."

"Finally, Vernon, he blows his engine. They back it down and next thing I know, they're under that car working on it. Like they didn't do a thing to cause it."

She and Aggie chuckled. Mommaw drew on her cigarette and tapped ashes into the palm of her hand. My head had jerked up at the mention of my father, Vernon. But for a minute they'd stopped talking. I went to the refrigerator with a glass and poured milk. Before I took it to the table, I hunkered down and watched the pilot flame under the refrigerator. No matter how many times I watched, I could never catch it flaring. I didn't understand how a gas flame kept food cold. I settled back at the table, careful to make a good milk mustache.

"Least, he didn't want to know how much money Warren brings home. They ain't nothing left after they take out the taxes as it is. That and by the time the bootlegger gets his share." She leaned forward, cigarette dangling from her lip, and slapped her knee with her free hand, cupping the hand with ashes so as not to accidentally blow them around. She removed the cigarette from her mouth. Smoke roiled in all directions.

"Yeah," Aggie said as she continued cutting hair.

"You know, he asked me how many kids I had. Said he weren't going to tax them. He just wanted to know." Mommaw laughed again. "I said I'd had six, and none of them home anymore."

I burped after I'd finished my milk. Mommaw looked sideways at me. I grinned.

"Cathy, get in the freezer and get a package of hamburger out to thaw for supper."

I hopped down from my chair and went over to the huge chest freezer that had sat on the side of the kitchen forever. On top of the freezer sat a clear glass bowl filled with plastic fruit, mostly grapes. I took that off and put it on the table and lifted the freezer's coffin-like lid. My cousin Terry told me once deep freezers like this one would hold dead people while their coffins were being built. He said they'd kept my great-grandfather in the freezer when he died because it'd snowed so deep the dead-people-takers couldn't get here till the next day. My mom always said Terry told fibs. I looked down inside the huge chest. On the bottom lay a package of hamburger. All the way down. I'd have to get a chair. Mommaw was doing her occasional counting of all her kids and what they were doing.

"Roy works at the same place as Warren. Vernon, he works over in Ravenswood at a 'luminum plant. Gay and Faye married . . . Faye's still in Florida . . ."

I dragged a chair over in front of the freezer, climbed up on it, and slowly lifted the lid. Now how could I reach the bottom and hold the lid? I decided if I bent one arm backward and held the lid, half my body could slide down into the freezer, then I could reach with the other hand and get back out without being trapped. I felt cold air on my skin and wondered what it would be like to be dead and trapped inside. I pictured myself lying stretched out on the bottom. It'd be quiet, I thought. My arm began to hurt, so I pulled myself up and out of the freezer, along with the package of hamburger.

As I climbed down off the chair, Mommaw said, "So many died of the croup back then. You almost died too, didn't you, Cathy?"

"What's that, Mommaw?"

"I said you almost died of the croup, too."

"I forget."

She laughed and said, "You was only about one year old."

I put the hamburger on the sink and went back to the table.

"Aggie, you remember?"

"Sure do." She was still cutting hair, and I noticed there wasn't much hair left. Many blue tufts lay on the towel. I thought maybe someday my hair would turn blue. After all, hers had once been black, like her eyes. Well, almost black. Dark brown.

"You know I told Jean the other day she was looking a might wormy. She needs to dose herself."

"My mom?" I knew it had to be because my Aunt Jean had died. But with Mommaw talking, you had to hang on to her words. She'd talk about one thing then jump off on another.

"Yeah, your mommy," she answered. Now Aggie was combing the blue hair from front to back. She mumbled about getting it even. She picked up the scissors.

"Tell me about when I almost died of croup." I moved closer so I could hear the story better. I was trying to decide if I'd had enough cookies.

"Oh, you heard this before. You was turning blue, and I fried up onions and put 'em on your chest. You cleared right up. Why, your mommy was sure you were going to die. That doctor wouldn't even come up here and see to you. I had to do something."

I didn't say anything, but Aggie said "I'll swan" again. I reached over and got me two more cookies.

"You about through cutting my hair?" she asked Aggie.

"Yeah, I reckon." Aggie put the scissors down and looked over her handiwork. Mommaw patted her hair but didn't seem to notice there wasn't much to pat. She got up from her chair, folding the towel she'd had around her shoulders, and went to the refrigerator, opening the door to stare a while at the mostly bare shelves.

"Ain't much in here to go with hamburger. I'll go out to the cellar and get a jar of beans, maybe pickles. I'll fry patties, and we can eat it on bread with pepper and mayonnaise. How'd that be?" she asked me.

"That's my favorite! I'm hungry!" I answered while rubbing crumbs from around my mouth.

"You staying, Aggie?"

"No. I got to get home. My man'll be coming in."

They said their good-byes, and Mommaw fussed around the kitchen, cleaning up, waiting for the hamburger to thaw. She didn't talk, and I rearranged the fruit in the bowl on the freezer, squeezing the plastic grapes, which always popped back into shape.

Later, when supper was ready and we were sitting down to eat hamburgers with sliced pickles and canned corn on the side, the back door opened, and Poppaw came through. He staggered in and sat at the end of the table. Mommaw rushed around and fixed him a plate, removing the pickle and corn from hers and putting it on his, along with the last hamburger.

Poppaw ate his food, and when he finished, he burped as he got up from the table, and without a word went to the bathroom. I heard him peeing really loud. He came out and went on into the bedroom and fell into bed.

Mommaw washed dishes, and I sat at the table and played with my dolls. I heard the refrigerator whoosh on. I sighed. I'd missed it again. It was quiet in the house. *Not much goes on around here*, I thought. *Not since I'd recovered from the membrane croup.*

# AWAKENING . . .

# CHAPTER 8

# WHAT WE CALLED HOME

I WAS READY TO GO into the first grade, although I was only five. I could count, a little, and knew a few of my letters. Mom read to me all the time, so I figured this school thing would be easy. I was excited that I'd get to walk by myself from our apartment four blocks away to Central Elementary. Mrs. Lenear was my first-grade teacher, and she was so pretty. I was smitten with her, but that didn't keep me out of trouble. I wasn't in school long before she had to tell me several times to "hush." One day, turned around talking to Sandy behind me, I felt my desk, with me in it, move out of the row and back against the wall. Ms. Lenear meant business. I behaved the rest of the year, for the most part. I remember the staying-too-long-at-the-pencil-sharpener incident, but my parents never found out about it.

I fell in love with a boy named Danny. He had red hair and freckles, and I thought he was the cutest boy in the class until I saw that his ears were dirty. Walter loved me, so Jane had told me, but I didn't feel the same way. I don't remember asking my mother why Walter's palms were so white while the rest of him was so dark, but she tells me I did.

One day, on the playground, I walked in front of the swing set. All of a sudden I felt myself flying through the air when

I got kicked in the head. The next thing I remember was sitting on the couch in my living room dressed only in my slip. A sixth-grader had walked me home, they told me. I went back to school the next day with a bump on the side of my head and decided to walk way around the swings.

****

The summer between first and second grade we moved out of the apartment and into a tiny house. It only had one bedroom, so once again I slept on the couch. This little white house sat in the yard behind the landlady's house, with another just like it across from it. Mom said to my Aunt Norma it was nothing but a storage building but "it's all we can afford." I thought it was just my size. I had a big neighborhood to play in with sidewalks for my bike and a new school, North Point Grade School. The cooks fixed the best food: navy beans, cornbread, spaghetti, chocolate pudding. Mrs. Schools, my second-grade teacher, taught us drawing and painting.

School always smelled like chalk and oiled wooden floors. All the windows reached up to the ceiling and were covered with dark green shades. In the winter we built snowmen over by the slicky slide and got our rubber boots and mittens confused in the cloak rooms, one for girls and one for boys, where we hung our coats and hats. In warm weather we played red rover, jumped rope, double Dutch, and I loved to play tag, running until I got a stitch in my side.

When we returned from recess one afternoon in Mrs. Grimm's third-grade class, the principal had come in. He gave each of us silver dog tags on a beaded chain. My tags were engraved with my name and address. They jangled around my neck when I flew to the sky on the swing set or tickled my nose when I hung upside down on the monkey bars. I wasn't clear on why they were given to us, but I do remember Mrs. Grimm saying, "Just in case we need to identify you." I asked Dad about it, and all he said was something mysterious: "Cuban Missile Crisis."

In the summer when school was out, we neighborhood kids loved to chase the ice cream truck, clutching two dimes in our sweaty hands for an ice cream cone. At nightfall, we had contests to see who caught the most fireflies. On hot days, I went to the swimming pool if one of my friend's mothers would drive. Mom didn't drive.

On summer days, I left the house early in the morning and returned to eat lunch then was gone again until after dark, when we'd all hear our names called out by our mothers to come home, time for supper or bed. Pedaling fast against the dark, I'd fly home to smells of meatloaf and freshly made biscuits. After dinner was television, *I Love Lucy* or *The Flintstones*. Our front door faced west, and I remember standing to watch the sun set between the huge maple and oak trees across the street.

\*\*\*\*

Every summer when I'd go stay with my grandparents, my Mommaw, expecting it to get really hot, cut my blonde hair into a pixie cut. She said cutting it tight around my face brought out my pretty green eyes with their long lashes. "You look like your grandmother put a bowl on your head," Mom would always say when she got me back from a visit. My first-grade picture shows my Mommaw's hair cutting-talents. On the other hand, my second-grade picture shows my skills—with a razor, anyway. The night before the school photos, I'd discovered my Mom's razor, and shaved off half of one of my eyebrows. I caught wooly worms to put on my eyebrows to replace mine, but the worms crawled off right away.

During the summer, Mommaw would take me and a cousin or two up to the camp my parents owned on Williams River, way over on the other side of the state from where we lived, where the mountains are. We'd pile in the back of my grandparents' pickup for the three-hour drive, with a blanket over us to keep us warm. We loved when our hair stood straight up from the wind, and our blanket flapped almost out of our hands.

The camp was a tiny, three-room cinder-block house in a field with a half dozen other camps and within walking distance of the Williams River, where we'd wade in the shallow water. It didn't have a bathroom, and it was scary going out to the outhouse. I'd heard noises down one of the holes before. I asked Mommaw about it, and she said it was probably some fool possum.

****

After a year or so, we moved out of our tiny house a few blocks over into a little white house with two bedrooms. Finally, I had a room of my own. My room had twin beds, so I had one, and my growing collection of stuffed animals had the other. Between my bedroom and my parents' bedroom was the bathroom that had a huge claw-footed tub. During bath time, I'd sink down in the deep tub, hook my toes on the faucet and float. In the hall, in front of the bathroom, was a big floor furnace. In the winter, the furnace made whooshing noises when the gas flared. It was heaven to feel the warm air flowing into my room.

We had lived in this house about a year when one night I was playing on the floor beneath my chest of drawers. I thought I'd grow up and be a famous actress, so to get ready, I pretended with my dolls. I was lying on my back, my dolls on my belly, one foot propped up on the chest of drawers. A movement from the corner of my eye drew my attention to the chest. It was tilting toward me and was going to fall, squashing me. I stiffened my leg and the chest wobbled back. A few small items on the top slid off, landing to the side of my head, but nothing hit me. I didn't play under the chest again, but I never figured out how it came to tilt. It sat deep and square and even on the floor. One day, I approached it, intending to dig out socks and underwear when I grabbed it and shook it. It was heavy and wouldn't tilt no matter how hard I tried.

Once, I lay on the couch in the living room, my old, yellow baby blanket over my legs. I was watching television when I felt a cold draft on my feet. I looked to see the blanket rising in the air, as if someone invisible was pinching the blanket between two fingers to get a peek at my toes. I sat up to get a better look when it suddenly dropped back down. The only vent in the house was the hall furnace, which was several feet away. No windows were open. Mom was in the kitchen washing dishes, and Dad was at work.

Nervous and unable to stay put, I got up and went to the front door to watch the neighborhood. Suddenly, a huge bolt of orange lightning flashed across the sky. It branched and forked and flickered for a long time before disappearing. I looked for clouds. There were none. Then suddenly, another huge, branched lightning bolt blazed across the sky. It flicked its end as if it were sticking its tongue out at the setting sun.

The strange lightning was on the news—no one knew what caused it. And I didn't tell my parents about the things moving around in the house. I felt as if everything was going to go wrong.

# CHAPTER 9

# FROM A TIME BEFORE

MOMMAW HAD COME TO VISIT my home in Point Pleasant, a little river town next to the Ohio. She and I were on the back porch, and I watched as she hulled strawberries. Suddenly, I looked at her, confused. I knew this scene had happened before: the porch, her, me, the strawberries, the hulling. But it hadn't really happened. She'd never been to this house we'd just moved to—only to the apartment and the little tiny hut. So how could I remember?

I said to her, "All this has happened before, Mommaw. I remember it."

"What's happened before?"

"You on this porch with the strawberries. Me standing here. But you haven't been here before."

She kept hulling berries. "Well, you probably lived before, and you're just remembering it," she said.

"Lived before?"

"I reckon. How else would you remember?" This time she raised her head and smiled at me as a strawberry dropped into a white glass bowl.

"I don't know," I said. "If I lived before, who was I?"

"Oh, I suspect you were a little girl, pretty much like you

are now. You went to school, and you had a puppy dog." She returned to hulling.

"Not a kitten?"

"Well, maybe." She paused, her hand with the paring knife balanced on the bowl's rim.

"You want a kitten? Then you probably had a kitten." She chuckled, "I'll bet you were rich and ate strawberries every day." She popped a slice into her mouth. She rose, bowl in hand, to go in the kitchen.

"Do you remember what it was like when you lived before?" I asked as I followed her into the house.

"No. If I did, I'm sure I just continued on, same old thing, over and over." She smiled down at me.

*Same thing over and over?* "Really?" I asked.

She dumped the strawberries into a colander and set it in the sink. She paused and thought a moment. "Well, maybe I was rich. Maybe I lived in a big house, owned a big car, and was married to a movie star."

"Not married to Poppaw?"

"Well . . ." She rolled the strawberries around and around in the colander, the cool water splashing over them. She stopped and looked out the window. I waited. And waited.

She never did answer me.

# CHAPTER 10

# NIGHT LIGHT

LITTLE WHITE MISSILES FROM DANDELION blossoms floated through the air and past my head as I pulled my red wagon toward the edge of my grandparents' backyard. I began searching through the grass under the Grimes golden apple tree for fallen tent caterpillars. The silly things fell to the ground as they wiggled in and out of their tent city. I looked up to see thousands of them as they bustled about, bent on stripping the tree of leaves. Many times I stood at a distance and watched Poppaw light a torch and set fire to the gossamer webs. That day, I knew this particular tent I trundled under was slated for destruction, as I had overheard my grandparents' battle plan. I hurried to collect as many caterpillars as I could and put them in my wagon for a ride out of the yard and a stay of execution.

Handling the caterpillars was a treat. Their many legs tickled my skin and their "fur" felt soft to the touch. Mostly brown, with a streak of blue down its side, a caterpillar would turn this way or that, wanting to escape my hand. They would fall and land on grass or the concrete walk, but they crawled away as fast as their legs could go, anywhere but in my direction. I looked up to see Mommaw watching me. She called out to family working or playing in the yard to come see. Now I looked at where she pointed. As I had put two caterpillars in the wagon, one crawled out. She laughed and said I never seemed to notice my collection of caterpillars grew smaller as I moved about the yard.

But I pulled my wagon with my dwindling caterpillar supply to the creek. I hoped they could swim to safety as I tossed several at a time into the water.

Nighttime was coming, so I pulled my wagon onto the covered porch in front of the cellar until the next day. It was getting late, and relatives who lived nearby began to drift home.

Bedtime came whenever I got sleepy and tolerated having the day's grime washed off me before climbing in bed. This night, I was too awake, so I went into the cellar in search of an empty canning jar and a lid. Then I went into the kitchen, intending to rummage in the junk drawer for Mommaw's small hammer and nails. Poppaw sat at his usual place at the end of the table. He tipped his whiskey bottle and then chased that gulp with a swig of beer. He watched me passing, Mason jar clutched to my chest.

"Where ya going, Stinker?"

"Going out to catch lightning bugs, Poppaw."

He laughed, as he always did, as if I had said something funny, and then he went into a coughing spasm. I thought he was going to choke. Finally, he straightened and shook a cigarette out of the pack from his shirt pocket. He lit it with his Zippo and sucked in the smoke. I found the hammer and nail and scooted outside, but I heard him wheezing as I moved away from the door. I put the hammer and nail on a metal table in the backyard and took the jar and un-poked lid to begin my hunt.

Dew lay heavy on the grass after a sun-drenched day. It was quiet in the backyard, except for a few crickets and tree peepers. When it got completely dark, I kept bumping into the lawn chairs. The dew made my bare feet cold and wet. I looked up. No moon, but the fireflies lit up trees like lights strung for Christmas. My plan was to catch enough bugs to use like a flashlight.

Tiny lights blinked on and off near me. I ran after the bugs that always seemed to be just a little bit higher than I could jump, but I soon had three in my jar. I clapped on the lid to keep them safe as I looked for more.

I heard a car coming up the driveway and ran to the side of the house to see who it was. An uncle got out, a big shape moving in the dark, and stumbled toward the back door. I didn't speak. I turned so he couldn't see my glowing lightning bugs.

The screen door's springs made a loud *sprang!* when my uncle jerked it open, and he tripped over the top step. A few moments later, I heard his and Poppaw's voices faintly. I moved farther into the yard in search of more bugs. Suddenly, a loud scraping noise like a chair being pushed across the kitchen floor caused me to run to watch through the screen door. Poppaw and my uncle stood beside the table, facing one another, fists clenched. Each swayed as if in a good wind. Then Poppaw shoved my uncle's shoulder, who swung a fist at my Poppaw and missed.

The big men grabbed one another's shoulders and began struggling, trying to bring the other to the floor. They turned and tussled toward the door, toward me. I scrambled off the steps and back into the yard. The screen door slammed back against the house as both men stumbled off the concrete steps and onto the sidewalk. They were big, dark shapes. I heard grunting, feet scuffling. A shout drew my eyes toward the back door where I saw Mommaw framed in the kitchen light.

"For God's sake, stop it!" she shouted.

But the giants didn't stop. Blows from fists met flesh, as they oomphed and grunted. Mommaw stepped out into the black night, hesitating a moment, then ran in the direction of the men. As dark as it was, her white blouse glowed. I watched her movements as she bobbed between the two men. I heard the smack of fist on skin. This time, it was Mommaw who grunted.

My eyes adjusted more to the darkness. The two giants froze, panting. Mommaw ran into the light from the doorway and hopped up on the steps. She glanced back at the men and then stepped into the kitchen, pulling the screen door away from the back of the house where it had stuck. She slammed it shut.

The two tottered into the rectangle of light spilling from the kitchen. Poppaw's shirt hung out of his pants and his hair stood straight up. His glasses were gone. He opened the screen door and hung onto the door frame to drag himself back into the kitchen. My uncle, just as messy, waited a moment before he too grabbed the screen door to step into the kitchen.

I was still standing with my jar clutched to my chest. My bare feet ached with cold. I stepped onto the sidewalk, still warm from the day's sun. I scraped my feet to remove clinging grass blades. I went over and peeped in the door. Each man slumped at opposite ends of the table. Poppaw roused enough to pick up the whiskey bottle and take a drink. I stepped back to the sidewalk, not sure if I wanted to go inside. The dark pressed against my back like a big heavy monster—it seemed as if it were breathing down my neck. But I remained, waiting for my feet to dry. My grandmother would fuss at me if I tracked grass into her clean house.

Behind me, the monster eased, and I again noticed the sound of crickets. I heard the rumble of men's voices as they talked to one another, a steady tone reaching my ears like distant thunder. A shuffle of feet from table to refrigerator and the thunk of bottle tops being snapped off beer were the only other sounds in the kitchen.

I needed to pee. I needed to set my lightning bugs down. I was tired of clutching the jar to my chest.

I slipped the screen door open quietly, hoping no one would notice. I stepped into the kitchen. Poppaw's big head turned toward me.

"'Bout time for you to go to bed, huh Stinker?"

"Yeah, Poppaw. I'm going."

"Taking your lightning bugs, too?"

"Yeah, Poppaw." I forced myself to walk slowly. My uncle had his head down on his arms on top of the table. I thought he was asleep. Poppaw's head dropped down on his chest, and I moved out of the room.

I tiptoed into Mommaw's bedroom. She was a dark shape under the covers. I heard her snoring. I hesitated at the door, the fireflies glowing in turns in my jar. Then I went to my bedroom and changed into my pajamas. I remembered I needed to go to the bathroom, but I'd have to pass again through the kitchen.

I got into bed, sliding beneath cool sheets, hoping I'd shed all the grass blades first. I stared up at the ceiling for a long time. I turned my head to the bedside table and watched the fireflies slam against the jar sides trying to get out. I'd forgotten to punch holes in the jar lid. I fell asleep, but it seemed only a few moments later when the early morning sun woke me up, just barely peeping through my window.

When I looked at the fireflies, they lay still at the bottom of the jar. Their glow was gone.

# CHAPTER 11

# CICADA BUZZ

THE BACK DOOR STOOD OPEN, the morning sun warming the kitchen. The sound of buzzing cicadas drifted through the screen door. A dragonfly floated by my narrowed screened view on its flight to the creek. It would join a few crawdads and hundreds of minnows. The grass on the creek bank might hide a brown snake, which slithers away quickly if you step beside it. Patches, my grandmother's calico cat, came to the backdoor mewing. She had taken a break from her new litter of kittens, probably piled sleeping in an old cardboard box in the smokehouse. No one in the kitchen answered her or let her in. She wandered away, probably to find a mouse or vole. I stood on a stool at the sink washing canning jars and lid rings. At eight, I was finally old enough to help with canning.

At the table, my grandmother peeled apples. She was almost finished with a deep red Rome when her knife sliced down to a dark bruise. Watching her peel good apple away from the bad spot, I made a face, scrunched up my nose. *Nasty!* I was thinking. She sliced the apple down to the core, threw the core onto the paper, along with the bruise. The good parts lay in a metal colander.

"Doesn't a dark spot ruin the apple?" I asked her. She chuckled, never lifting her eyes from the next apple she was peeling. "No," she answered and shook her head. "There's always bad parts. Got the good with the bad. Just the way it is." Tilting her head to the side, she eyed the next apple she had picked up, cut half away, and discarded the other half, all bruised.

The water in the white porcelain sink was almost too hot to bear. My hands were deeply reddened as I dipped the jars and rings and soaped them with a blue dish rag. I then slipped them into cool rinse water in the other sink bowl. I sat them upside down to drain on a towel at the sink's edge. When I looked at the back door through the jars' sides, the scene outside sparkled and shimmered.

As the morning deepened, the heat in the kitchen rose. I felt a bead of sweat slip down the middle of my back. My aunt came into the kitchen through the back door. Her trip to the cellar netted a dozen more jars. She set the box with the jars and rings on the other side of the sink. I plucked them out and began washing again. "The water is ready," she told my grandmother. She meant the tub of water on the old gas stove out in the smokehouse. The stove is from the 1920s, green with long white knobs, black, spidery-like burners, and a warming oven on top. They only used it for canning, and working in the cooler smokehouse brought relief from the hot kitchen. "The water is boiling," my aunt repeated as she pushed open the screen door, turning toward the smokehouse.

Scalding jars and rings was not a chore I was old enough to do, my grandmother had told me. Her sister Rose had lost a toddler girl to a tub of scalding water when she fell in it. Rose still grieves. *If the little girl had lived, she'd be my parents' ages*, I thought.

I washed the jars and rings, adding them to the two dozen I'd already washed. I climbed down off the stool and went to the refrigerator and pulled out the copper-colored, metal pitcher to pour an ice-cold glass of water. I noticed a Mason jar of clear liquid in the refrigerator door. "What is this?" I asked my grandmother. She looked up briefly to see what I was pointing to. "Oh, that's your poppaw's. It's moonshine. Don't ever drink from that." I stared at it a moment then shut the door. "Didn't you give me some, Mommaw, when I was sick?" "Yes," she said, "a bit. With honey in it. Only because you had a cold. Just a little."

The water in my glass from the metal pitcher was so cold it made the top of my nose hurt. My aunt returned with a galvanized tub and gathered clean jars to take to their scalding. I helped her load them, but I remained in the kitchen after she and my grandmother went to the smokehouse, with the peeled apples loaded into a large soup pot to cook them on the old stove. I sat down on the cool linoleum, sipped my cold water, and with my damp finger traced the colored spots of paint my grandmother had splattered on the floor. The base coat was "battleship" grey, she told me. The spots were yellow, red, cream, and blue. It was the current style, she said. Since she couldn't afford new linoleum, she'd painted over the old.

A pressure cooker on the stove cooked the evening's supper. Roast beef. My grandmother liked the meat fall-apart tender. It takes a lot to feed the men, she said. She meant my grandfather, my older boy cousins, maybe an uncle or two who had wandered in. My mom was amazed my grandmother fed the men first and then the women and children ate what was left.

My grandmother never considered changing the order in which she fed people. It was an old custom, Mom said.

The cicadas buzzed nonstop. I once asked my grandmother what cicadas were. "They're ugly bugs," she told me. "Similar to grasshoppers and locusts. They eat trees. The buzzing is for finding mates. After that," she continued, "they split out of their shells and leave them everywhere." I knew about those. I found their crinkly forms stuck to trees and clothesline poles. I collected them and lined them on the window-sill of my room.

From where I sat on the floor, I studied the oak table and chairs. I saw a piece of gum stuck under the table. Probably Terry did that. The chest freezer set against the wall beyond the table suddenly clicked on and hummed. On the freezer lid, two glass ashtrays sitting close to each other rattled and tinkled. When no one was looking, I'd sneak burnt matches out of the ash trays and eat the sulphurous-tasting heads.

The gas-fired refrigerator added heat to the room when it kicked on, but it was silent. My eyes roamed farther around the room, and I caught a glimpse of color in the medicine cabinet mirror hanging on the wall beside the refrigerator. I saw the reflection of the chestnut trees at the edge of the backyard. Another dragonfly hovered in the air just beyond the backdoor. Then it was gone.

Over the sink, the two windows were open, and a breeze came through and ruffled the white curtains. It quickly died down, but not before I noticed the curtain almost tumbled a small green planter with ivy into the sink. I leaned against the stove where on top the pressure cooker peeped steam from time to time. Near the backdoor sat the oak buffet where my grandmother kept her pots and pans. Her bills were in the drawer. A kitchen safe matching the table and chairs sat against the wall behind the table, and inside were my grandmother's dishes, salt and pepper shakers, coins in a small dish, and a jar with her gallstones. They were the size of marbles.

I couldn't see the clock on the stove, the only one in the room, but I figured it was about 10 a.m. I knew my grandmother was hoping to finish the day's canning before afternoon when it got even hotter. She came through the back door just then and sat down at the table. She began peeling more apples, occasionally eating a slice. I got up and approached her. I studied her blue hair and her black glasses frames. She pursed her lips as she peeled. She suddenly looked up at me and smiled. Stretching out her hand, she offered me a slice of apple from the edge of her knife. I leaned in toward the blade, taking the slice in my teeth.

It was sweet and tart, firm and cool to my tongue.

# AWARENESS . . .

# CHAPTER 12

# I SPY

"I SPY SOMETHING GREEN," MOM said as she looked all around the room to throw me off.

"The plants?"

"Nope."

"Hmmm. The book on the coffee table?"

"Nope."

Several more guesses of green objects in the room got a "no" response.

"Give up?" She inhaled her cigarette deeply and blew the smoke toward the ceiling.

"Okay. I give up. You win. What's green?"

"Your eyes." She grinned at me. Smoke circled into her brown hair.

"No fair! I can't see my eyes!" I frowned, crossing my arms over my chest. But I soon grinned back at her. Mom loved to fool me.

"Want to play rummy?" I asked.

"Did you do your homework?"

"Yep. Mrs. Grimm held me in at lunchtime today, and we went over my times threes. I think I get it now."

"You're lucky. I never was too good at math. Go get the cards, and I'll get out the cookies."

"Great!" I ran to get the playing cards. I was better at rummy than at I spy.

But luck was not with me in rummy. "Tomorrow!" I'd crowed, as Mom bustled around the room setting my stuffed animals to rights on the other twin bed. I had changed into my pajamas and hopped into my bed. "I lost today, but I'll win the next time!"

"We'll see about tomorrow," she said as she came toward me and tucked the covers under my chin.

"I'm going to win at rummy for sure!"

"Think so, huh? Well, we'll see. You have to do your homework first, though. After dinner, too." She patted me and smiled. "Put your little head down on the chop block," she said. She sat down on my bed and recited another favorite rhyme.

"Alas and alack! I left my britches on the railroad track. Along came a train, choo choo choo, and cut my britches half in two!"

"Oh Mom! I'm too old for that!"

Laughing, she patted my arm, got up from my bed, and moved toward the doorway. I was sure my mom was the funniest mom of anyone else in my class.

"Wait! Sing me a song."

"Aren't you too old for *that*? No, it's time for you to sleep. You'll never get up in the morning for school."

Mom snapped the light off, and I snuggled down under my covers.

****

Now, I was home from school, ready for rummy. I plopped my books on my bed, and I rounded the door from my room into the living room and headed to the kitchen, where my Mom always seemed to be.

"Mom?"

She moved toward the stove and answered me without turning. "I'm making your father's favorite this evening." She lifted a pan from the stove, clapped a lid on it, and drained the potato water into the sink by tilting the lid on the pan. Hot starchy liquid streamed out without losing a single potato piece. *Mashed potatoes! My favorite, too!*

"And what else?" I asked as she lifted the hand mixer to the pot. "Oh, baked steak, fresh green beans, biscuits, and ice cream for dessert."

"Oooh, Sounds good. Why are you fixing Dad's favorite?"

"He says his stomach sours when he's working midnights. When he came off his last midnights, he's still complaining about his stomach. I thought maybe if I fixed his favorite he'd feel like eating."

"Can I help?"

"No, you go on in and watch cartoons. He's supposed to be home for dinner." The hand mixer began to whirr.

But he wasn't home in a half hour. He wasn't home all evening. She and I ate with our plates balanced on our laps and watched the news on television. I knew better than to ask to play a game.

The next morning, Mom fixed my breakfast and gave me lunch money before I walked to school. I came home in the afternoon and noticed no supper cooking on the stove.

I sat down at the kitchen table and played with the salt and pepper shakers. She was washing dishes, staring out the window over the sink.

"I'm hungry," I said.

"What do you want? I'll fix whatever you want."

"Macaroni and cheese."

She baked it in the oven, just the way I liked it. But she didn't eat. She watched me eat, her cigarette smoke making the air in the kitchen a blue haze. She also watched the backdoor, and soon she was standing, staring out the door's glass pane to the backyard. When she wasn't inhaling on her cigarette, she picked at the loose skin on her lips. I watched television after doing my homework.

Later, I heard her moving around the kitchen, washing, drying the dishes, putting them away. Tired of television, I came to the kitchen door to see her standing at the back door, again watching through the glass in the upper half of the door.

I didn't need to ask why. She was watching for Dad. The setting sun shot rays of golden light on her face, softening the sharpness of her cheekbones. I noticed the fine blonde hairs on her cheeks.

The next day was Friday. Again, the same thing. No supper on the table. Mom busied herself in the kitchen, but I didn't ask for anything to eat.

I turned, walked out of the kitchen and through the living room to the front porch of our small, white house on the corner of Twenty-Fourth Street and Madison. I kept my bike at the end of the porch past the swing. I steered it toward and down the steps and into the front yard, on out into the street. I rode my bike every day, and I was proud of the fact it was my cousin Bobby's bike, a hand-me-down. A boy's bike. I deemed it faster than a girl's bike, but my girlfriends didn't think so.

I pedaled up the small hill on Madison and turned around at

the top, intending to ride it back down, hands free. My friend Cheryl called to me from her yard before I could begin.

"Hey, Cat! Let's ride over on Mount Vernon. Maybe go down to Harmon Park."

We took off, biking the rest of Madison, to Lincoln Avenue, then to Twenty-Second Street, then right onto Mount Vernon, in the direction of town. The houses were a bit nicer on that street. Mrs. Grimm lived in the brick house on the left. She was determined I'd learn the times table before school was out. I hoped so.

We rode through Harmon Park, past the ball fields. We stopped to watch a softball game for a while. "Let's go toward the railroad bridge," Cheryl suggested. It wasn't often I rode that far, but I agreed. It was a warm, clear evening with plenty of daylight left. Once on the sidewalk, heading toward downtown, we passed a beer joint, the Dew Drop Inn. It was then I spotted a car. A 1957 robin's egg blue Chevy, just like my dad's. I liked it better than the old grey Oldsmobile he used to drive. But he'd wrecked it a couple years earlier. Mom said he fell asleep behind the wheel. "He'll have to pay that man's hospital bills," I overheard Mom say to Aunt Norma. I wasn't clear on all the details, but Dad had to have surgery on his knee. The glove box lid had come down and nearly cut off his leg. He had hobbled around on crutches for several weeks.

I slowed my bike on the sidewalk as we passed the Dew Drop. Cheryl, not aware I'd slowed, continued ahead of me. I stopped and dropped one foot on the pavement to steady my bike, one thigh resting on the crossbar. I couldn't see in the window. The glass appeared to be black. Just then the door opened. Sitting on a stool at the end of a bar was a man who looked like my dad. He didn't look up, but was staring down into a glass on the counter in front of him. Just two seconds I saw him; then the door closed. I hesitated a bit but hopped back on the seat of my bike and began pedaling fast to catch up with Cheryl.

Just before dark, I came into the house.

"Where have you been?" Mom asked. She was in the living room, the television on, smoke rising from her cigarette.

"Out on my bike with Cheryl."

"I was beginning to worry. Don't go off again without telling me where you're going."

I sat on the couch and pretended I was interested in the *Jack Benny Show* on television.

The phone rang. It was my Aunt Norma. I half listened to Mom's side of the conversation, then listened more closely when I heard her mention my dad.

"I don't know where on God's green earth the man is. He slept till noon on Thursday then took off. He hasn't been home for two days . . . No, I didn't call . . . What good would that do? I can't go get him . . . No, I'm not going to call Wanda. Jack won't drive me to the beer joint. What would I do anyway if I did find him? He's not going to come home . . . No, I don't need anything. I got plenty of cigarettes last time I was at the store . . . No, he's on long break. I just hope to God I see him before work on Wednesday."

I turned back to Jack Benny and listened to him laugh and joke with George Burns and Gracie Allen. Toward the end of the show, Mom told my aunt goodbye and hung up the phone. She lit another cigarette. She watched the end of the show, and when it went off, she crushed out her cigarette and went into the kitchen.

I followed. She turned toward me. "Did you have any dinner?"

"No."

"What do you want?"

"Ummm . . . Macaroni and cheese."

"Again?"

"Yeah." She got a pot out of the cabinet and filled it with water, then set it on the stove, turning the knob until a flame caught under the pot.

"Mom?"

"What?"

"Wanna play I spy?"

"No, I don't think so. I'm not in the mood."

"I spied something you might want to know."

"No, I don't think so. Did you do your homework?"

"I don't have any. It's Friday."

"Go take your bath while I wait for the water to boil. We might as well eat. It doesn't look like your father is going to come home again. God only knows where he is. Why in God's name does he do this to me?" She grumbled that last part as she went to the cabinet and reached for the box of macaroni noodles. She turned and hesitated, looking at me. I was playing with the salt and pepper shakers.

"What'd you spy?"

"Nothing." I shrugged. "I'll go take my bath."

"Dinner will be ready when you get out."

After my bath, I put on my pajamas and came into the kitchen. A single bowl of macaroni and cheese sat on the table. A plate with white bread piled on it sat beside it and also a small dish of applesauce with cinnamon and sugar sprinkled on it. I glanced over to see Mom standing at the kitchen door again. Cigarette smoke wreathed her head. She picked at her bottom lip with her fingernails. I watched her stare out into the dark backyard as I ate.

Then suddenly her whole upper body expanded as she drew in a deep breath, paused just a moment, and then she exhaled slowly through her nose, shoulders sagging. Her breath fogged the glass in the backdoor, capturing her sigh for all to see.

# CHAPTER 13

# SHELTER

BUILT ON THE WALLS OF a cinder-block cellar, above spiderwebs, jars of pole beans, crocks of pickled corn, and baskets of russet potatoes, was the cellar house. It stood up the hill a few dozen feet behind my grandparents' house.

Tin roofed and painted white, its trim buttercup yellow, it had two windows. It also had two doors, but one opened to air because the thirteen, silvery wooden steps had been removed when the wood grew rotten. But that was after my mother had once fallen down those stairs. As she tumbled from top to bottom, her grip on me loosened, and my two-year-old body sailed through the air. I landed on my head, suffering a bump behind my ear.

As I grew older, but still a child, I often sought the solitude and comfort of the cellar house. My family used it as a storage room, but over the years, different family members had stayed in it. Whenever I went up there, I'd dig down in an old hump-backed trunk full of *Mutt and Jeff* comic books, past scraps of quilting fabric, to my dad's army uniform at the bottom. Along with the uniform was a dark woolen quilt I needed to snuggle under. It had been pieced by my great-grandmother. She had cut, pieced, and quilted material that she had saved from old suits and overcoats, building a durable cover to last several life-times.

The only furniture in the cellar house was an old, white iron bedstead. It was three-quarter size and had belonged to my great-grandparents. Atop the bed was a feather mattress (of blueticking) sewn by my great-grandmother and stuffed with duck feathers and down.

Plucking the wool quilt from the trunk, I'd run and plunge into the tick that was puffed high on the iron bed like a loaf of yeast bread ready to go in the oven. I'd sink into the mattress and be startled for a few seconds, thinking there was no bottom. Falling down into the dark and quiet, I'd pull that scratchy quilt over myself like a monk needing a hair shirt, and I'd hope for a rowdy thunderstorm. Some days, my hopes came true.

First, the wind would come up, and trees would moan and whisper in response. Faintly at first, I would hear the thunder rumble. Then the thunder's timbre deepened and boomed and rattled the glass in the windows. Lightning flashed so bright I saw it through my eyelids. From my safe place, swaddled in ticking and wool, I let the fear take over.

Rain began its hesitant patter, then built with the wind to a solid crescendo. Deeper I'd sink into the tick, drifting down to where no one and nothing but me belonged. Then the wind calmed, and the rain settled down to its most serious business. It echoed and drummed with such an intensity I thought it would surely pound through the tin roof, sluice through wool and flesh and bone—bearing traces of me on through tick and iron and wood—splash down to the cellar below, to webs and beans and potatoes and nasty pickled corn, and then dribble onto the concrete floor. Then it'd seep out through the walls at the base of the cellar, into the dark, rich soil. It'd flow by the earthworms and grubs and moles, down to the water table and into the well. It'd get drawn up in a tin bucket, cold and pure as melted glacier ice.

I'd lie still for the whole time it rained, from first splatters on the roof, to torrent, and to the steady drip from the eaves to silence. And in the stillness, I'd throw back the quilt and rub the blotches on my bare legs and arms from the scratchy wool.

I'd clamber out of the tick, throw open the door, and inhale the ozone, and listen. Then I heard the faint cries of the tree peepers in the rain-swollen creek. They'd chorus louder and louder.

Calling for someone to love them.

# CHAPTER 14

# BACK HOME

PENNSYLVANIA AVENUE HEADS OUT OF Saint Albans to the countryside. Still within the city limits, the old farms out that way are mostly given over to neighborhoods. Just off that road in the 1930s, my mother and her siblings were born and lived on a farm. One day, when I was around nine or so, my mother, my aunt Norma, and I went out Pennsylvania, crossed the railroad tracks in my aunt's Rambler, and drove as far into a field as we dared, to see the house where my mother and her family had lived all those years ago. We got out of the Rambler and walked up a hill, the day warming from a bright sun, the trees dazzling the eyes with fall colors.

It was squirrel season. Mindful of avid hunters in the woods and listening for shots to ring out, we stepped through high weeds, picking up stickle burrs on our socks and pants legs. Gaining another small hill, we spotted the house of my mother's childhood sitting forlornly in the middle of a field. "It's a lot smaller than I remember it." My mother paused to catch her breath, hand on her chest, puffing. Her cheeks were red from the effort of her walking.

"Look at that, Norma. Do you remember it that way?"

"No. Don't seem like it was that small." Norma walked

closer, watching the house as if it would disappear into thin air. I followed, my mother bringing up the rear. As we approached the two-story white house, it was obvious it hadn't been lived in for many years. The front porch was rotting away, falling down. With no front door, we glimpsed curing tobacco leaves hanging in bunches from the ceiling's wooden beams.

"They've made it into a barn!" My mother stood, mouth open, her brow wrinkled. I noticed she had a burr in her soft curly hair. I was pondering how a burr got in my mother's hair when my aunt, ever the realistic one, said, "Whadya expect? That someone still lived here? Why would they? It's in the middle of nowhere."

My mother had regained her breath and walked around to the side. "Watch out for snakes, Cathy," she warned me as I followed. She stopped to stare up at the roof.

"Norma, now that I think about it, how did Herman and Alex get up on that roof at Christmas?"

"I don't know, but they did. I heard those sleigh bells, same as you did."

They were talking about a story often told to me by my mother. When she and her sisters were little girls, their mother had their older brothers climb up on the roof on Christmas Eve, making the girls believe it was Santa Claus.

"It was our signal to get to bed," Norma added. "Santa was coming, and if we didn't get to bed right then, he wouldn't bring us gifts."

"He didn't bring us much anyway. There wouldn't be nothing but oranges and nuts in our stockings," my mother said as she walked around to the back of the house. "No wonder, though. Mom with ten kids, and that no-good daddy of ours gambled all the money away." Her pedal pushers exposed her white legs, turning red from the bright sun. My aunt, darker in complexion—she got the Cherokee coloring, and Mom got the Irish, Mom had often told me—didn't seem as bothered by the heat or the sun.

"I remember Fay got a doll once. I don't know how come she got one and we didn't," Norma said then looked down at the ground. "Remember, we'd find hoofprints in the snow the next morning outside our window." My aunt turned to me. "We were sure they were Santa's reindeer hoofprints. But they were really our draft horses."

My mother studied the house. "There sure were good times in this house, though, weren't there, Norma? Of course, you remember how Mom used to cure us of the earache? Blow cigar smoke in our ears. I used to get earaches every winter. We never went to the doctor back then. And you and me used to have to go get the cow every evening so she could be milked. It's a wonder we didn't get snake bit. I used to lift up rocks on purpose to see if I could find one." I was surprised at that bit of information.

"You? Lifted up rocks looking for snakes?" I asked, amazed this woman who cautioned me every time I went out the door to play would do such a thing.

My mother laughed and fished a pack of cigarettes out of her pants pocket. "Yeah, I guess I did. Times were different then, though." She picked out a cigarette, pulled a matchbox out from the cellophane of the cigarette packet, extracted a match, and scratched it to life on the side of the box. Lighting her cigarette, she inhaled deeply as she studied the house.

"Kenny did get hurt pretty bad one time, remember? He was

cutting firewood, trying to earn twenty-five cents to go to the movies. He missed with the axe and nearly cut his foot in two," Norma said, bumming a cigarette off my mother. Norma rarely smoked.

"That's right. I remember. Mom ran to the next house down the road, it's gone now, and got the neighbor to give her a chaw of tobacco. Mom chewed that stuff and by the time she got back to Kenny, it was good and wet. He had laid the axe through the top of his foot. She soaked it in a tub of water, then pushed the wound back together and slapped the wet tobacco on it. It didn't get infected. It was supposed to draw the poison out." Seeing my eyes apparently ready to pop out of my head, she continued, "No one could afford a doctor. You made do with the old remedies. Lots of times, they worked."

"God, it's a wonder we didn't all die," my aunt said, shaking her head. We wandered around the old house a little more, peering in windows. The floors were rotted throughout. The living-room fireplace was as my mother had described where all the kids would sit as each one in turn plucked dried corn from an iron skillet sitting in the ashes. The way she'd described eating cracked corn in the dead of winter made it seem like the best thing ever. As for me, I thought it actually sounded kind of hard, dry, and burnt. I preferred Jiffy Pop.

We hadn't been able to see into the kitchen because the back door was closed. The rear porch was rotted away as well. But my mother had talked often of the meals that had come from the wood-burning cookstove, the table laden with food fresh from the garden, all cooked in lard or bacon grease.

Suddenly, the sound of a shotgun rang out nearby. We took it as a signal to head back to the car. The three of us walked a little more quickly back through the weeds, over the hills, and back to the road.

Once in the car, headed toward home, my mother continued talking about her family, as if she could bring them to life inside the car.

"One of my earliest memories was my mother having a miscarriage. I saw Daddy take the axe from the outbuilding into the house to put under her bed. That was to take away the pain of the miscarriage, but it didn't seem to help because she screamed for a while; then she just moaned, seemed like for hours. Me and Norma—you remember, Norma?—hid up in the apple tree in the front yard, waiting for it to all be over. I don't remember what they did with the baby, but I remember Daddy carrying something out in his hands. It looked like a bloody towel. I guess he buried it in the backyard."

She turned to me in the backseat. "Norma and me talked a language all our own, like twins do . . ."

"She's two years older than me," my aunt interjected, turning from the wheel to grin at me.

"Anyway," my mother frowned and continued, "we stayed up in trees for most of the summers when it was daylight and time to play outside. We'd chatter away in a language no one else understood but the two of us."

Mom cracked her window and turned to Norma. "You remember Mom telling us that when Fay was born, she was premature. She had to carry her around on a pillow she was so tiny. She kept her in a dresser drawer. And Wanda, she nearly died when she was a kid." She turned to me again. "She was the last one and the most sickest. Her spleen burst. They had to do surgery to remove it. At that time, must have been around 1949, they didn't think you could live without your spleen. But she had been throwing up blood for years, big old clots. Her belly was big like you see those kids suffering from malnutrition."

Her voice faded out for me. Hot and tired from the walk, I realized the burrs I'd picked off my clothes were sweaty in my hand because I didn't have anywhere to put them. The rhythm of the car as it traveled back down Route 60 rocked me, helping my drowsiness along. I stretched out on the backseat and watched as the sunlight flashed off and on the car's ceiling when we passed under trees, just as images of my mother's young life flashed through my mind.

I imagined the house as it used to be. I pictured her and Norma up in the apple tree in the front yard jabbering in a language no one else knew. I had no brothers or sisters, and my cousins served only occasionally as company, so I didn't know exactly what it was like. No one had ever gone up on the roof to play Santa Claus for me, ringing bells and ho-ho-hoing. Mom lost her mother when she was only ten. I wasn't ten yet, and I hoped I wouldn't lose my mother. I loved her soft hair and pretty blue eyes. I loved the way she made my favorite foods and bought me pretty dresses from the Sears catalog for school each year.

The flashing light on the car's ceiling coupled with the heat of the day made staying awake difficult. I pinned her stories to my mind, and as I fell asleep I imagined my mother and me, two happy little blond girls, holding hands and running through a field.

# CHAPTER 15

# DEVIL FACES

Sweat pooled under my neck and soaked into my pillow. Despite the heat of the room—I'd heard Mom say it wasn't supposed to dip below eighty degrees all night long—I held the sheet up to my neck. The window in my room was open with a screen at the bottom. No street light shown through my window, but a faint light glowed, probably coming from a disappearing moon.

Suddenly, a dark head jutted out from inside my closet, just past the door. I stiffened, holding my breath. Why hadn't I shut the closet door? I always did at night, because I knew the faces would stick out at me if I didn't. Their faces weren't clear, but they—five of them—thrust out one after the other. Then they were gone. I let out the breath I'd been holding, pulling the sheet even tighter to my chin. Tears slid down my cheeks. I had nowhere to go. I had run to my parents' bedroom before when this had happened, woke them up. They told me to go back to bed, that nothing was there. I was dreaming.

I called them the devil faces. They had horns sprouting from their foreheads, or at least what I saw in the dim light. I thought maybe they had big noses and long, sharp teeth. They were evil. I couldn't see their eyes, but I knew they were looking at me.

I watched the closet, trembling. One jutted out again and then the other four fast and then all pulled back just as fast into the closet. I struggled to swallow with a dry throat, squinting in the direction of the door. I forced my eyelids to pop open. If I didn't watch, they might thrust themselves at me closer. *I've got to get up and close the closet door! As long as the door is closed, I'm safe.* I couldn't move.

The problem with that plan was whatever was under the bed. I only knew it was evil. If my arm flopped over the side, it might grab me with its cold, slimy hand. If I got out of the bed, it'd grab my leg and pull me under. It'd eat me. My mom would come in to my room in the morning to wake me to go to school and I would be gone. Eaten.

Another face jutted out—closer that time! I let out a small scream and pulled the sheets up over my head. Just then my bed moved. It jerked away from the wall, and my whole body jiggled when it suddenly halted to a stop.

I don't remember anything else till morning when Mom woke me up.

"Hey, sleepyhead. Time to get up and get ready for school. Come on. Let's go!" I gazed at her still half asleep but then I remembered. I looked at the closet door. It was shut. "Did you close my closet door?"

Mom was straightening the stuffed animals over on the other twin bed. She didn't turn as she answered, "No, I didn't." Then she did turn and look at my bed. "Why did you move your bed away from the wall?" She moved toward the end of my bed and scooted it, with me in it, back against the wall. "Did you lose a toy behind there?"

"No."

She patted my feet and smiled at me. "Hop to it, Hop Sing!"

"Mom?"

"Yes?" She was fussing with clothes on my dresser, putting them in the drawers.

"Do you think . . ."

"Do I think what, honey?" She continued folding and tucking items.

"Never mind."

"Well, get up, or you're going to be late for school. I've got your cereal laid out, the milk and sugar. What are you going to wear today?"

"Wear?"

"How about your blue shorts and red and blue top that goes with them? I think you have clean socks in here," she said as she opened and rummaged around in the fourth drawer.

"You took a bath last night, didn't you?" She didn't give me time to answer. She put my clothes, neatly folded, on the other bed and went out.

I stayed where I was, the sheet up to my neck. Another morning tired and sleepy. I hated the nights when I forgot to shut my closet door. Why had my bed moved? Was it the devil faces? Had they moved me? Then they were getting too close. Who closed the door?

Finally, I scrambled out of the bed, tangling in the sheets. I dressed and went into the kitchen where Mom was. She didn't turn from the stove. I stood and watched her back. The sun was shining through the glass in the backdoor. Dust motes floated in the sunlight. Mom clattered dishes, and a bunch of silverware she'd just washed crashed into the drainer. Over the noise, I heard her singing.

"And His hands were nailed pierced for me . . ." Her beautiful alto voice trailed off. Then she turned.

"There's your cereal. Pour you a bowl." I didn't move.

"What's wrong?" she asked.

I slipped into the chair at the end of the table, picked up the cereal box and poured it in my bowl. I added lots of sugar and then the milk. I started eating. She began singing again. She reached for her dish towel and smiled at me, came over, and kissed me on top of the head.

"Did you sleep good?" She asked as she sailed out of the kitchen. She didn't wait for an answer.

I slipped out of my chair, went into my bedroom, slowly, slowly. Everything was where it should be, the toys, the jewelry box on my chest of drawers. The sun came in the window, and dust motes danced in this room, too. The closet door remained closed. I headed toward the bathroom to brush my hair and teeth.

I hoped and hoped all day at school to remember to close the closet door before I got in bed. That night, after taking my bath and putting on my pajamas, I went over to the closet door. I stared at it, willing the thing to seal shut. I got in my bed. Mom came in and over to the side of my bed. She sat down. I smelled her sweet smell.

"Put your little head down on the chop block," she said as she leaned over and kissed my forehead. She got up, went to the door, and turned out my light. Slowly, my eyes adjusted to the darkness.

I looked over toward the closet. The door was open.

# CHAPTER 16

# SOMETHING GATHERED 'ROUND ME

I STOPPED DEAD IN MY tracks.

Oh my God. What is that?

Mom was in the kitchen. I threw my books down on the couch and headed toward her. She was lifting the lid on a pot, stirring the contents. The steam rising caused her to step back, then replace the lid. She looked at me.

"What's wrong?"

"What is that thing in the living room?"

"It's a Christmas tree. Don't you like it?"

"It's silver. It's metal."

"Yeah. Your dad got it at work. Kaiser offered them at a discount to their employees. It sure is a lot less messy. I hated the needles that always fall off a real tree. Everyone's getting these silver trees now."

"But I want a real tree."

"Well, we have this one. You'll have to get used to it. You'll have to admit the bulbs look pretty on it."

"I don't know."

"Sorry. It's here to stay."

She lifted the lid on the pot again.

"Dinner will be ready in a couple hours when your dad gets

home. I'm making fudge, too." Mom's peanut butter fudge was the best. It usually didn't set up, and I got to eat it with a spoon, but it was the best way. For a long time, I thought that was the way all fudge was eaten.

I turned and went back into the living room to get my books to take them to my room. I glared at the tree. Well, it was shiny, I had to admit. I liked shiny things.

After dinner, I lay under the tree, looking at the packages. One box had my name on it.

"What's in this?" I asked Mom, who was watching television.

"Guess."

We did this every Christmas. Santa, Mom had explained long ago, left off packages early as he had too many to deliver these days on Christmas Eve. I'd been told three years earlier by my cousin Randy that Santa Claus didn't exist, but I liked thinking he still left gifts early to reduce his delivery load. My favorite part of Christmas had become the guessing game Mom and I played.

"Umm, it's a jewelry box."

"Nope."

"Give me clues."

"Okay. It's purple and has eight sides."

"An octopus!"

"How could it be an octopus? It'd die in there."

"An eight-sided jewelry box."

"No, I already said it wasn't a jewelry box."

"I need one, though. My cedar box is full."

"Guess again."

I gave a few more guesses, but she said I didn't come close. Then it was time for bed. I got up and went over to the crèche on top of the television. Mom didn't decorate much for Christmas, and I'd only just made the crèche in school. I brought it home before Christmas break. I moved the small ceramic Joseph a bit closer to baby Jesus in the manger. Mary was poised at the head of the manger. I couldn't afford any animals to add to my cardboard crèche, so it was just the three of them. Sort of like Mom, Dad, and me.

It was still a couple days before Christmas, and I woke and went into the living room to see Mom had added "pom poms," she called them, at the ends of the branches. I had no idea what they were supposed to imitate on that silver thing. I watched as the lamplight in the room reflected off the metal "needles," trying to find a way to like it. As usual I admired my distorted image in the red bulbs—the ones with the verses from "Silent Night" printed on them. I tried my best to warm up to the silver tree. I was convinced every kid sang carols with her family, had big dinners with turkey and mashed potatoes and big, fat rolls, then played games, listened for Santa on the roof, too excited to go to bed—just like I'd seen on television. Then they'd get up Christmas morning and gather around a real Christmas tree. And all I had was a metal one. A stupid metal tree.

"Quit feeling sorry for yourself," Mom told me after finding me standing, staring at the monstrosity for the umpteenth time. "Lots of kids don't even have that."

**** 

Christmas Eve came, and Mom clinked dishes and banged pots and pans in the kitchen. However, she fixed TV dinners, and we ate on TV trays in front of the television. I wondered what all the dish and pan noise was, since the dinners went from freezer to oven, but I didn't ask. Dark came early, and the evening stretched out before me, alone on the couch as Mom retreated to the kitchen again. The dish clinking and the pot and pan clanging were louder this time. I was watching cartoons. It was near my bedtime when Dad came home. Mom appeared around the corner of the kitchen, dish towel in hand, but didn't say anything and didn't move as she watched him wrestle a huge box through the door.

The box was partially wrapped with Christmas paper—two different kinds. He staggered a bit as he shoved the box closer to the Christmas tree.

"What in the world is that?" Mom asked, flipping her towel from one hand to the other.

"It's a Christmas present for the Cat." He looked at me. I sat down on the floor near the tree.

"Norma wrapped it for me."

"What were you doing all the way down in Milton? Is that where you've been?"

"I went Christmas shopping, Jean. What's wrong with that?"

"I didn't know where you were." She leaned against the door frame.

He staggered toward her, then went past her to the kitchen. She followed. I knew what was coming. An argument. I got up and went into the bathroom to pee and then to my room to get into my pajamas. The whole time I heard their raised voices in the kitchen. I didn't pick out words. I'd long ago decided I didn't want to hear what they were arguing about.

I hopped into bed, scattering stuffed animals, and I didn't give two hoots if monsters grabbed me and pulled me under the bed. I lay, not falling asleep until their voices fell to a drone. I drifted off.

A kind of strangled yelp, sharp and loud, brought me to sitting position in my bed, shocking me out of sleep.

"Vernon! My God!" It was my mom. Something bad was happening. I bounced out of bed, ran through the door, over the whooshing floor furnace, around the corner to the kitchen.

I watched what was happening, but my parents seemed to move in slow motion. I remembered Mrs. Grimm had told us just before we were dismissed for the holiday things would slow down if you were moving at the speed of light. At least, that was the theory she'd heard lately, but no one seemed positive yet. Dad was leaning over my mother's pristine, white enamel kitchen sink and throwing up blood. His face turned a deep purple as he strained and heaved. Drops of blood seemed to hover in midair before splashing all over the white surface.

Mom sat frozen at the table, her hand to her mouth. I came unfrozen and turned to run. Back in bed, I pulled the covers up to my neck. I could still hear my parents; Mom was clearly worried. Dad seemed to strangle and gasp.

****

The next thing I knew, it was dawn, or at least, very early in the morning. I opened my eyes to see a faint grey light coming through the window. I wasn't sure what woke me, but the first thing I became aware of was how silent it was. The furnace wasn't on, so the house was completely quiet. On our backstreet, few cars went by even in daylight, but especially on Christmas morning the streets were empty.

Then I heard my parents' gentle snoring from their bedroom

across the hall from mine. Moving to the foot of my bed on my knees, I looked out my window. It had snowed during the night. The cars, houses, trees, fences were covered with at least six inches of snow. Then I heard a train, its whistle muffled, the snow absorbing its blast, move past my town. Nothing else moved in the steel light—I saw the humps of cars in the street, trash cans, bushes. The houses dark still. The trees' limbs bowed with the weight of the snow, the power lines drooped. I stuck out my tongue and licked the cold window pane, then pressed my forehead against it, rocking it back and forth on the glass.

Images of Dad throwing up into the sink flashed in my mind. My mom wringing her hands. Her face scrunched up, her eyes full of tears. I thought about the silver tree. Then my mind turned to the times Dad came home at supper time, and we'd eat. In the summertime he'd give me dimes for the ice cream truck. Occasionally, we'd take a drive, even taking the hour's drive to see my grandparents or to my Aunt Norma's for a visit. Then drive back late, the car's windows down, me lost in the huge backseat of the Oldsmobile as we drove back to Point Pleasant on Route 35. Once in a while, I'd catch the smell of cow manure when we passed the dairy farms. A few cars rocketed past us going the other way. Then again the image of Dad's blood, splashing against the brilliant white of Mom's sink.

I'm not sure how long I stayed still, or when I sensed I wasn't alone. Whatever it was, it was behind me. I thought of the devil faces from my closet, the things that lived under my bed that would grab me if an arm or a leg flopped over the edge.

I froze, barely breathing. My heartbeat thundered in my ears.

Then suddenly I was warm. A warmth settled around me,

like a big person hugging me or someone laying a blanket over my shoulders.

I don't know how long I knelt at the end of my bed. My mind seemed to have emptied, but then all of a sudden I knew things. I heard no voice, but images came into my mind, all jumbled, none clear. I seemed to know more than I did before, but I didn't understand.

I had no words to describe any of it, but suddenly I knew everything was going to be okay. I would not be like my parents when I grew up. I would have a different life.

My breathing became rapid as the warmth dissipated, but rather than feel sad, I felt happy. I felt joy. I knew it was joy, though I had never used the word for myself or anyone else. It was just a word in a Christmas carol till then.

Hardly able to believe what had happened—whatever it was—I could not stay still. I wiggled off the bed, past the blankets, and jumped to the floor. I raced to the living room.

Without calling to my parents, I skidded to a stop on my knees under the tree and grabbed a present. I tore through the paper. Ah! So this was the eight-sided, purple thing! A box of bath powders!

By the time my parents heard and shuffled in, half asleep, I was almost through opening my gifts. I grinned at my parents.

"I'm gonna open the big box now, Dad."

He laughed. "Okay," and reached for his pack of cigarettes on the coffee table.

I ripped off the paper and struggled to open the top of the box.

"Need my knife?" He asked.

"No, I got it."

Down inside the box was a huge stuffed dog. It was gold. A poodle.

"Thanks for the dog, Dad. I think I'll name him Frenchie because he's a poodle." It was nearly as big as I.

"I'm glad you like it."

Mom went into the kitchen, and soon the smell of coffee wafted into the living room. I was reading the last page on one of my new books, just to see how it came out. I decided *The Moonstone Castle Mystery* would be a good read, and I could probably finish it before school started. Sitting cross-legged, I listened to my parents' quiet talk in the kitchen as they sat and sipped their coffee. Cigarette smoke drifted out into the living room.

"Vern, you have to stop this."

"I know Jean. I know." I heard his heavy sigh. Then my mom's sigh just before she got up, her chair making a scooting noise. I heard coffee pouring into her cup. She sat down again.

"You're not going to get over this, Vern. It's killing you."

Silence. Just smoke rolling through the kitchen door.

I glanced up at the metal tree, and the sun popped between dark snow clouds, shining through the window onto the metal needles. I felt a brief flash of the warmth that had snuggled me earlier. I would be all right. It was like a promise, one I could trust.

Shifting my gaze, I noticed a red bulb's words, "All is calm," as it gently rotated on its branch. I leaned in, watching my reflection distort and my nose get as big as an old bloodhound's or Rudolph's. I smiled at my reflection, and it glowed back at me.

# CHAPTER 17

# HOUSE OF LEAVES

DENISE LEANED OVER TO STRAIGHTEN the room wall. She stood back up, hands on hips to survey her work.

"Not bad," she nodded her head. "Wait! Don't we need a window over there?" She pointed to the left.

"Probably a good idea unless you want the baby in a dark room," I suggested. I moved to the left side of the house and kicked leaves aside to create an opening in the wall. "That oughta do it."

"Did you ask Ricky to be the dad?" Denise asked, watching me as I straightened a kitchen wall.

"No. I thought you did."

"Where is he?"

"Don't know. Last I saw him he was on the slide."

"You wanna go ask him?"

"No. He seems to talk to you, but he never says anything to me."

"Okay. I'll be right back. You guard the house."

Denise walked away past the swing set and toward the slide to find Ricky. I had a crush on him, but he seemed to like Denise. It was just one of those things. I thought he was really cute with blond hair and blue eyes. Seems like I only attracted

Dwight or Dwayne—I could never tell which boy was which because they were identical twins. I only knew the one who liked me chased me across the road to my house, beating me over the head with his books. At least Mom explained that meant he liked me. I took her word for it, but his book pounding hurt. I'd told our teacher about it, but like all teachers did when a student complained, she just shrugged and told me to work it out.

Denise and Ricky came toward me.

"Okay. What am I supposed to do?" Ricky came around to where I was to look at our leaf house. "This is a house? I thought you had a big cardboard box. This ain't no house."

"Yes it is," I answered. "Can't you see the rooms? This here's the front door," I said, gesturing toward the line of leaves with a gap in them. Ricky looked at the lines of leaves Denise and I had gathered; four rooms were neatly mapped out on the pea gravel, each with door and window openings.

"This is stupid. I ain't playing no house with a bunch of leaves on the ground."

Denise moved to straighten one of the walls. "Fine, Ricky. Go back to playing on the slide for all I care." He hesitated. He shoved his hands in his pockets.

"Okay. What I gotta do?"

"Well, you have to go to work. Then you come home, and we feed you dinner."

"Who you two playing?"

"Denise and I are both the wifes. We couldn't decide who was supposed to be the wife this time, so we're both gonna do it."

"That ain't right," Ricky said, kicking a house wall a bit.

"There can only be one wife. And ain't there supposed to be kids? Where's the kids?"

"This is our house, and we make up the rules," I said, using my foot to kick the house wall back in place. "Becky said she'd be the baby."

"Ain't never heard of no girl making the rules." Ricky stepped into the front room, the one we designated the living room. "Where's the kitchen? Where we supposed to eat?"

"I haven't cooked yet," Denise said. "I'll go find Becky. You go to work, Ricky."

"What am I supposed to be doing?"

"Well, what does your dad do?"

"He drives a truck."

"Well, then. Do that." Denise stalked off to find Becky. I knew she was getting tired of explaining things to Ricky. But really, boys didn't know anything about house, I'd noticed. They played tag, red rover, football, and wrestled on the ground till the teachers broke them apart. Their favorite game, though, seemed to be baseball.

"I'm gonna be a professional baseball player," Ricky announced as if he heard my thoughts.

"Can you make money at that?" I asked.

Ricky turned toward me and gave me a look I was used to: dumb old girl. "You bet! I heard DiMaggio made tons of money. That's what I want to do." He started swinging an imaginary bat.

"Fine. Just get out and go work. I gotta clean house. You're messing it up."

"I am not!" He kicked the front wall again. He ran off to the middle of the playground. Another boy walked up to him, and they both started swinging imaginary bats.

"Do we need him?" I asked Denise when she came back with Becky in tow. I pointed toward Ricky, now running around imaginary bases.

"No, probably not. We can just pretend and probably do a whole lot better." She turned to Becky, who, without a word, walked through the front door and then to the back room on the left, where the baby's room was.

"I don't think we need boys. They don't do anything but play, make a mess."

"Well, let's just pretend our husband has come home. You wanna cook, or you wanna clean?"

I moved to the room we'd designated as the kitchen. "I'll cook, you clean. I know! Let's pretend Rock Hudson is our husband! He's cute."

"No, how about John Wayne?"

Disgusted, I put my hands on my hips. "John Wayne? He's an old cowboy."

"Well, he's handsome. At least my mom thinks so."

"I know, let's choose both!"

"That's perfect! We got one who's good looking and one who's probably a good worker. What are you gonna fix for dinner?"

Just then a strong breeze came up. It blew our hair around, then lifted the hems of our dresses.

"It's a dust devil!" I shouted, looking at the leaves at our feet begin to gravitate upward.

"What's a dust devil?" Denise asked, grabbing handfuls of leaves, trying desperately to put them back in place. But it was no use. The dust devil was strong as it moved through our house. Becky stood stock-still, as leaves whirled up around her ankles then up under her dress. She screamed and grabbed the hem of her dress, shoving it back down. Then it lifted her hair straight up. I thought for a minute it'd lift her off the ground, but it didn't. I was disappointed.

Seconds later, it was gone, moving over to the center of the playground where Ricky was batting again. He stopped long enough to lift his arms out from his body, enjoying the wind playing around him. It didn't lift him, either.

We looked at our house of leaves. It was destroyed. Becky took off, and just then, the recess bell rang. Denise and I shrugged at one another and moved toward the school to go back to our rooms.

"We could build a new house tomorrow," I suggested.

"Yeah. I guess so. It shouldn't be too hard. This time, let's make six rooms. How many husbands do you want?"

"Let's make it four—two for you and two for me."

"Yeah, maybe one of them will work and make good money." We had reached the inside of the school building, and she turned to the right to go to Mrs. Jewel's room. I turned left to go to Mrs. Jarrett's.

"Yeah. Let's get ones who are worth something."

"Okay!" Denise went through her room doorway. Ricky popped through the door behind her.

I went into my classroom and moved toward my desk. *Boys. They sure were cute, but they weren't good for much. Wonder how Mom stands it. How does any girl stand it?*

But Rock Hudson sure was cute, I had to admit. Maybe one day I'd marry him, and he'd make a good husband.

# CHAPTER 18

# PLUNDER

Rᴀɪɴ ᴘᴏᴜɴᴅᴇᴅ ʜᴀʀᴅ ᴏɴ ᴛʜᴇ tin roof. It had started while I was reading *Bobbsey Twins at the Shore*. I was a little old for the book—well, at least I felt so at ten years old—but it was the only one I found after coming to my grandparents to stay for the weekend.

I finished the book and listened for sounds above the rain. The house was quiet. Poppaw was at work, so I got off the couch to go find my grandmother. The TV room was next to the kitchen, but she wasn't cooking or cleaning. Maybe she was doing laundry out in the smokehouse where the washer was. No, that didn't make sense. It was raining, so she couldn't hang clothes on the line. Noting her pack of cigarettes that always sat on the buffet if she was in the house was gone, I figured she was across the road at Gertrude's house.

With no one around, it was a chance to plunder. Grabbing a couple cookies, I went into my grandparents' bedroom at the back of the house. The light in all the rooms was dim coming through the gloom from outside. I didn't turn on the overhead light or lamp. I went to the dresser drawer and opened the drawer on the top to the far right. Ah! The cigar box, just where I knew it'd be. I took it out and sat down on the bed and opened it.

Biting into a cookie, I lifted the photo on top. In it, two men stood wearing cowboy clothes. The leather pants weren't complete—chaps I think I'd heard them called—and these had fringe up and down the sides. They both had gun holsters and cowboy hats. One had a gun in his hand. They smiled at the camera. No writing on the back, so I'd have to remember to ask my grandmother if she knew who they were. I laid it aside and took out the next.

It was a wedding photo of my grandparents, so my grandmother had told me. She wore a plaid coat that fell to mid-knee. Her hair—so dark I imagined it must have been blue-black—was cut at an angle on her cheek. She stood slightly sideways to my grandfather, who wore a light-colored suit and had round-rimmed glasses. His hair appeared to be blond. Neither smiled for the camera.

I must remember to ask my grandmother why she didn't wear a traditional white gown. I didn't know where they'd married. My father, I knew, was born a few months later.

Next was my favorite photo. My grandfather stood squarely facing the camera. He had on the kind of pants worn when riding horses, a black leather jacket, and a cap, pulled low onto his forehead. He had a cigarette dangling from his mouth. My grandmother stood to his side, slightly facing him, away from the camera. She wore a light-colored dress that was just above her knees. She had on white socks and black Mary Jane shoes. Her hair slanted at an angle, so it must have been around the time of their wedding. Her right arm was raised, resting on his shoulder. I thought he looked strong and even mean, but I thought she looked like a little girl. She was so pretty.

A noise brought my head up from digging in the cigar box.

I put it aside, taking another bite of cookie, and made my way toward the kitchen. The rain had stopped, but the clouds kept everything dim. The kitchen was empty. I looked out the back door and peered out the window over the kitchen sink, but no cars had pulled into the driveway. My grandfather had not come home yet. I glanced at the clock. He was late.

I took another couple cookies and returned to the bedroom to continue looking at photos. I heard thunder rumble overhead; then it deepened enough to rattle the windows. A blurred photo of my grandparents' house made me realize it was once a dark color. It'd been white for as long as I remembered. In this photo, my dad, a few of his siblings and cousins sat on the porch steps, on banisters, and on the swing, which was on the opposite side from where it was now.

Next was a framed photo of my dad's cousin, Virgil. So this was the famous photo that had fallen from the wall when my great-grandmother, Ida Mae, had died. I only found out about the photo falling much later. "No one bumped it," Mom had said. "That's right," Mommaw agreed. "No one was near it, but the minute Ida died, breathed her last breath, the photo fell.

"It's a mystery," Mommaw said. Once, I asked Mom about it again. "Did that happen?" I wanted to know. "Yes, it happened. We still don't know how it happened, but the photo fell the moment Ida died."

Now, here it was. That same photo in among my grandmother's photos. I touched it, thinking I might feel something. A vibration maybe? Virgil in the photo was a young boy, with perfectly white hair. My father had had white hair when he was small, too. They looked very similar.

Then another photo of my grandmother. In this one, she

was younger, maybe a young teenager. She sat on the arm of a chair. A nice-looking young man was sitting in the chair. My grandmother's hair, about shoulder length, was deep black. But it was her eyes that caught my attention. I didn't have words to describe the look on her face other than she looked so sad. Like she knew what was coming.

"What are you doing, plundering again?" I was startled at the voice, and the box of photos fell from my hands. I looked up to see my grandmother watching me in the doorway.

"Yeah, Mommaw. I love to look at your old photos."

"Well, put them away. Your daddy is coming to get you and take you home."

"But I was supposed to stay all weekend."

"I know. But your poppaw hasn't come home. I think it's best you go."

I looked up at my grandmother. She was leaning against the door frame, her face resting against one raised hand on the facing. I saw that look, just as in the photo. The same eyes as long ago.

# REACTION . . .

# CHAPTER 19

# ALARM CLOCK

"K-k-k-Katie, beautiful Katie, you're the only grr-grr-grr-girl that I adore! When the muh-muh-muh moon shines, over the ca-ca-ca-cowshed, I'll be waiting at the k-k-k-kitchen door!"

He was dreamy with those green eyes and bright blond hair. He had the voice of an angel, I thought as he leaned toward me in the next seat. And he was singing to me. No matter my name was Cathy, not Katie; it was close enough to melt my heart.

I was in love.

If he wasn't in love with me, he at least liked me. One week earlier, he'd given me his dog tags to wear, what all the guys gave girls who agreed to go steady. I was going to have a set made for myself to give to him. I'd lost my grade school ones long ago. I glanced down at his tags hanging around my neck: Nathan Taylor. Wow. I was going steady with Nathan Taylor.

The teacher dismissed our eighth-grade music class, which was the last class of the day. Nathan walked me to my bus. He gave me a quick peck on the cheek just as I was stepping on the first step into the bus. I quickly put my hand to my cheek. He grinned then turned and walked away. I found a seat and watched him weave his way among all the other school buses.

He disappeared around the end of one bus. He didn't turn to look back at me.

That was the last time I ever saw him.

*****

I thought the little white house we rented on Mt. Vernon Avenue was the best yet. We'd lived in several places since coming to Point Pleasant, but this one had a small backyard with a huge maple tree and a garage where my dad parked his car. Once again I had a room of my own, and it had a basement for Mom's washing machine and my toys packed in many boxes. Books were my favorites, and I often got those for Christmas, so they remained in my room in the bookcase headboard: *Great Expectations, Black Beauty, Old Joe,* and my Nancy Drew mysteries. The only toys I ever played with now were my horse statues.

I loved my room in winter; I'd lie in bed as a weak afternoon sun slanted into my window past the massive icicles hanging from the eaves. The most recent Nancy Drew mystery precariously propped on my tummy and a cup of hot cocoa made the winter not so dark or lonely.

When I arrived home, still feeling the tingle on my cheek where Nathan had kissed me, Mom was sitting at the kitchen table talking with my Aunt Norma. I knew immediately Mom was upset, although she didn't appear to be crying.

"What's wrong?" I stood in the kitchen watching the women, dreading what I was going to hear.

"We're moving in with Norma and Lloyd," Mom said. She tapped her cigarette into an ashtray on the kitchen table.

"Why?"

"Your dad is out of control. Haven't you noticed he hasn't been home?"

Of course I had noticed. "How long?" I asked.

"How long he's been gone?"

"No. How long will we be at Norma's?"

"We're not coming back."

She and Norma began talking adult stuff. I watched them. Neither woman looked toward me again. I turned to go to my room.

"Pack enough clothes to do you for the weekend," Mom called after me. "We'll come back for everything else later."

Not all my toys were originally in the basement. The third bedroom was my official toy room ever since we had moved one year earlier. Toys had been spread out all over the floor, but recently Mom had wanted to make that room into a sewing room, so she boxed up all my toys and moved them down into the basement. The only ones remaining upstairs were the few I had in my bedroom: a stuffed monkey with a yellow banana in his hand and an old ceramic doll an aunt gave me that she had received when she was a child. I also had a jewelry box into which I put Nathan's dog tags every night, and a cedar trinket box where I kept my prized stuffed real baby duck and a rabbit's foot.

My horse statues were all lined up on my headboard. The beautiful Palomino was in the lead with her colt. They would have to come with me. On my neatly made bed—the bed mom made every morning the second I got out of it—was my teddy bear Dad gave me when I was five and a few other odds and ends scattered about. My Barbie dolls, games, and all other sorts of toys were in the basement, and I considered briefly going down to get a few of those—just in case I wanted to play with them—although at twelve, that didn't happen much any-more.

I packed underwear, pajamas, socks, a pair of jeans and a couple tops, dresses for school, and my brand new brassiere, my very first, but I saved most of the space in my suitcase for my few toys.

"You ready?" my mother was at my room door. "Go pee before we go."

In the car, I heard the women talk about Dad, repeating stories of him going off on drunks, and how Mom had to call around to find out which beer joint he was in. She'd call his foreman at Kaiser Aluminum and tell them he was sick and not coming in.

I watched the hills out the car window as we sped by. Up on top of that hill, the tallest one around, what would I see if I were up there? The Kanawha River winding its way toward the Ohio, cows grazing, a real horse—mostly draft horses, but I did have one statue that was a draft horse—a Percheron. I saw photos of them in a magazine showing what the huge animals were. Had anyone walked on that tallest hill? Maybe if I walked up to the top, I'd be the first one to set foot on it. I liked the idea of being the first.

****

Once at my aunt's house, I lugged my suitcase into a back bedroom I was to share with my mother. I hung up my tops, jeans, and my school dresses then lay my underwear and pajamas on the dresser. I didn't know if I had a drawer where I should put my things. My cousins were in the living room. David was nine, and Joni was six. They invited me to go out bike riding around their neighborhood, which we did for most of the weekend.

On Monday, after David and Joni had left for school, I got in the car again with my aunt and my mother. We drove back to Point Pleasant to pack more things. I was planning to go down into the basement to get a few of my old toys. Joni played with Barbies, and maybe we could play with them together.

I lingered on the back porch, watching the children play on the grade school playground across the street. It had been nice living directly across from my school, but when it came time to go to junior high, I had to get on the bus to travel a few miles. I heard girls squealing as boys chased them. Some were swinging higher and higher on the swings. I remembered, swinging higher and higher until I felt I could escape gravity, as our teacher told us. When John Glenn orbited the Earth, she had brought her tiny television from home so we could watch the broadcast. I swung so high the chains jerked as I came back down, but I wasn't scared. I had gathered my strength and pulled hard on the chains to pump myself clean off the planet.

Just then I heard a noise. It was my mother in the house. It sounded like a scream—no it was more like a loud "Oh!" I ran inside.

The kitchen was littered with dirty dishes—in the sink, all over the table—still with food sitting in them. A half empty bottle of beer teetered precariously on the edge of the sink. I went on through to the living room, and I stopped at my bedroom door. My mother was standing with an alarm clock in her hand. It was crushed. It looked as if something heavy had been dropped on it.

"My God, Norma. How can anyone have the brute strength

to do this? He's crushed this." She looked at my bed. "He's slept in Cathy's bed."

That remark drew my eyes away from the clock in her hand. I saw that my bedcovers were twisted. The few items I'd left on my dresser were lying on the floor. I glanced in the bathroom, the only one the house had, and my bedroom was the one with direct access. I stepped into it and noted the towels on the floor, the whiskers in the sink, my dad's work clothes piled on the floor near the commode.

"What in God's name does he think he's doing?" my mother demanded.

"Jean, you know he's mad. He's mad you left."

"What was I supposed to do? I had no idea where he was. He was gone for days!"

"I know, Jean. I know. I'm just saying—he's mad."

"I'm going down in the basement to get my stuff," I said to them. Neither turned to look at me. Mom turned the clock over and over, as if it were my Magic 8 Ball. *Try again later.*

To get to the basement, you had to go out on the back porch and lift a hinged door in the floor to get to the stairs. I struggled with the door, dropping it a couple times before I finally opened it wide enough to rest it against the banister. I went down the damp stone steps into the inky blackness. At the bottom of the steps I knew a string hung down to pull to turn on the bare bulb. It was a cellar, really, I'd once heard my dad say. I pulled the string, and the light came on.

The basement was empty.

I twirled around. Then again. The bare stone walls glistened with sweat, but no boxes rested against them. No washer. No canning jars. No old, broken vacuum cleaner. Nothing but cobwebs and dust and sweat.

I ran back up the stairs to return to my bedroom.

"There's nothing in the basement," I blurted out. They turned to look at me. Mom was still holding the crushed clock.

"What?"

"It's empty! All my toys are gone!" Both women looked at me as if I were talking gibberish. Mom moved toward the door, and I was on her heels as Norma followed. When we got to the basement steps, we trooped down. I had left the light on. They both stood in the middle of the room circling, just like I had.

"My God . . ." my mother said. "He's even had my washing machine hauled off." She was fighting tears, running her hands through her hair as she twirled about. Shaking their heads, cursing my dad, they climbed back up the stairs. I moved to the middle of the dank, chilly room.

"Right there," I said out loud, "near that wall, was a large box, filled with my dolls. Barbies and all their clothes. A Ken doll, missing one arm. A friend gave me hers—an extra—because she said my Barbies shouldn't be without a Ken. Bride dolls—one was as tall as I was when I got it for Christmas a long time ago. I had Monopoly, Operation, Candy Land, and Clue. A bunch of decks of cards, Silly Putty, skates, stuffed animals, a huge box of crayons, and coloring books. And by the steps was a chair where I kept my Betsy-Wetsy doll with her bottle."

\*\*\*\*

Climbing out of the cellar, I looked toward the playground. The bell had rung, apparently, as no children were around. I stepped off the back porch and moved to look into the garage's window, hopeful for a minute. Inside were shelves filled with tools, and in the middle of the two-car garage was Dad's 1957

Chevy, which he rarely drove. He said it would become collectable. His arc-welding unit sat in one corner, and over in another were his fishing poles and tackle. He never put anything of his down in the basement. That was where anything belonging to me or my mother was stored.

Once back upstairs and in my bedroom, I began the task of packing a few more clothes in a box my mother had given me. I took pictures off the wall and added them to the top of the box. I was finished.

Leaving the house, we drove to my school. Classes were in session, so I didn't see any of my classmates. We went to the principal's office, where I sat beside the secretary's desk with my aunt while my mother went into the office to sign papers. I was to begin the new school, Hurricane Junior High, the next day.

I told my aunt I had to run to the bathroom, and she told me to hurry back. I left the office and headed directly to health class, where I knew my friend Denise would be. I pushed the door open slightly then slipped quietly into the darkened room and wasn't noticed by the teacher or the classmates. They were watching a film about the human reproductive system.

I saw Denise in the middle of a row of seats. I made my way over to her.

I leaned down, startling her as I whispered her name.

"What . . . Where you been?"

"I'm leaving the school," I whispered.

"What? What are you talking about?"

The teacher noticed us, now, but she only shushed us and turned back to the papers she was grading.

"My dad's been transferred. We have to move—now."

"Transferred? Where?"

"To Hurricane. I'll be going to Hurricane Junior High tomorrow." I dug in my pocket and brought out a folded piece of paper. "Can't explain now. I'll write you a letter." I handed her the note. "Give this to Nathan, would you? I don't have time to find him."

Denise took the note from me, hardly noticing it in her hand.

"You'll give it to him, won't you?"

"Yes, yes, I will. I don't understand. Why are you leaving now?"

"I'll explain later. I'll see you. We're not that far away. Maybe I can come back this summer and see you. Good bye." The teacher shushed again, louder. I turned to see her glaring at me.

"Okay. Bye." Denise whispered loudly. I turned and made my way back to the end of the aisle. The students I passed in front of remained intent on the screen in front of them, stretching their necks to see around me as I moved past. I glanced toward the screen. Wow. That's what a boy's penis looked like?

****

*Dear Nathan,*

*My dad has accepted a new job in Hurricane and we are moving. I wanted to see you before we left, but it was in a hurry. We're not even taking most of our stuff from our house. No room! It's a really good job. My mom will have her own car now.*

*I wish you luck on the history test but I know you'll do fine.*

*Maybe I'll see you this summer. I hope. Here are your dog tags back.*

*Goodbye.*

*Cat*

# CHAPTER 20

# MY CIVIC DUTY

Jennifer jumped up, spreading her legs, her hands clapping constantly. Her brown hair flew out and when she landed, she crouched down readying to jump again.

"Victory, Victory, we know how. We will win, and we'll say HOW!" She jumped up, spreading out her arms and legs, clapping again.

I was supposed to invent a cheer, but I had no clue how to do so. I'd never been a cheerleader, but I'd watched them at the games and imitated them at home on my own. Now, my cousin's girlfriend, a varsity cheerleader, was teaching me cheers and had come up with a new one I could use to try out the following week for the junior high squad.

She was selling me her skirt and sweater, too. That is, if I succeeded in becoming a cheerleader. I practiced constantly to ensure I did. Besides, I loved the physical activity of it. Granted, I didn't do backbends very well, but splits were no problem.

"You're about as ready as you'll ever be!" Jennifer said. I was catching a ride home with a girlfriend and her mother. She walked me to the street where I was to wait.

"Keep up the good work. Oh, here comes your ride. Remember the cheer?"

"Yeah, I think so. I've practiced it a lot . . ."

"Okay. See ya!" With a wave, she turned and headed back into her house.

\*\*\*\*

Tryouts were Monday afternoon, right after school. We were to meet on the football field where four teachers, plus our gym teacher, were the judges, already sitting on the bleachers. We would be called out one by one, and we didn't know the order. It turned out I was the third one called. I did the cheer I'd learned, then a split, a backbend, and a forward roll. The teachers thanked me, and that's when I saw my mother and my Aunt Norma in the stands. All I could do was wait on the field as the other girls tried out. Once everyone had had their chance, I made my way up to the bleachers to where my mom and aunt were sitting.

"Hi, guys. I didn't know you'd be here."

"I told you I didn't want you trying out, Cathy."

"I know Mom. But I wanted to."

"How are you going to get to the games? Your dad works shift work."

"I have girlfriends whose parents will give me rides to the games."

"What about the practices?"

"I'll find somebody. There won't be that many practices."

My Aunt Norma said nothing. Mom turned her head to stare out at the field.

She turned back and asked, "Where are you going to get the money for the outfit?"

"I don't know. I think it's only gonna cost about $40."

"Forty? We don't have that kind of money, Cathy."

"I have a little money saved. About nine dollars. I can use that."

"We'll see. They might not pick you anyway."

But they did. Five of us were chosen, and only one of us had been a cheerleader before. She was appointed head cheerleader. A good friend of hers was designated as the co-head, whatever that was.

****

Mom and I had been gone from our home for two months. Without a word of explanation to me or anyone else, she called Dad one day, and he came to my Aunt Norma's house to see her. He was dressed in khaki pants, a white dress shirt and shiny leather shoes. His hair was brushed back in an Elvis Presley pompadour. I'd never seen him look so handsome since I'd seen his army photos.

My aunt and I hung back in the kitchen while Mom and Dad talked in the living room. Norma was pouring coffee and puffing on one of her thin cigars. "She didn't have to call him," she muttered around the cigar. "She could stay here. Why does she want to go back?" I didn't know what to say. I didn't understand any of it.

Mom talked very little to me about the separation. The only thing new I'd learned from her since leaving Dad was that she'd left him once before when I was only a month old. She'd boarded a train and gone to Detroit, where another sister and her husband had moved. She stayed a month, and then we were back on the train and back to Dad. That's all she ever said about the whole thing.

The agreement, Mom told me later that night as I was getting into the bed I shared with her, was that Dad had agreed to move back in with us at a new house in Hurricane, near Norma. Mom wanted a sure way to get around to places other than the grocery store, which was mostly the only place he would drive her. He was not around to take her to yard sales and shopping, and if he had been, he had no interest in taking her to those places. Also, she would have family near, she said, but her own home. "All I ever wanted was my own home," she said as she combed her hair before climbing into bed. "My own home." She repeated as she turned out the bedside lamp. "Your dad will carpool the hour-and-a-half drive to Ravenswood."

Mom now had a ride to places, but I still didn't. Every game and every practice, I begged rides, and not once in that whole school year did Dad have to drive me. I didn't even ask him the time that my ride didn't show up. Dad was watching television in the living room. I watched him a few moments then went in to change my uniform. It turned out to be the only game I missed, something I was rather proud of.

****

On a cool October day, we students received word that of the three classes in the school, seventh, eighth, and ninth grades, our class, the ninth grade, was the only class not permitted to travel to Washington, D.C., for a class trip. We were too rowdy, they said. We were outraged. Several of us decided to stage a sit-in. We knew from the news that students were staging sit-ins all over the United States to protest unfair rules at their schools or laws of our government.

"No way," a couple friends said when the word spread about the sit-in. They didn't want to be expelled from school.

"They'd do that?" I asked.

"Don't you know it's your civic duty to behave?" one student said. "They catch you in a sit-in, you'll be thrown out as cheerleader."

I pondered that for a moment. They had chosen two alternates when they chose us five. If for any reason one or two of us couldn't perform our duties, we'd be replaced. *I would be replaced.* I felt a sudden jolt go through me. I'd watched the news shows enough to know that people were marching and sitting in to protest wrongs. I needed to stand up for something that mattered, even though my parents would never have the money for the trip.

It had cost me a good deal to be a cheerleader. The bumming of rides all the time was embarrassing, and often I had to go through several people before I found someone coming from my way. I lived outside of town, and that meant not as many people could give me a ride. So far, it had worked out.

The rules for cheerleading were strict: our hair had to be cut above our shoulders; we had to keep a 3.25 GPA; and we had to maintain a professional, respectful attitude at all times. Mom had given me the forty dollars for my outfit, but I panicked when the squad and our teacher leader wanted to add pompoms. I knew I'd never get the ten dollars for those. I spoke up and said I didn't think we really needed them. After all, that's what all the other squads did. Could we be different? I also couldn't afford the leg makeup, but Jennifer had given me half a bottle she said she didn't need. I used it every other game and only from the knees down. I hoped no one noticed when my skirt flew up during cheers.

The rest of the morning I thought about the coming sit-in. I couldn't back out. Lunchtime came, and then a couple classmates said it was time to file outside on the front lawn.

I came down the steps and over to my classmates. All sat cross-legged on the ground, not speaking, just sitting. I sat down in the second row. Minutes passed. No one came outside. I heard giggling behind me; then someone said, "Do they know we're out here?"

Then our principal appeared at the top of the steps. "You'd better get back to your classrooms, students. If you don't, I'll suspend every one of you."

With no hesitation, we all rose, went up the steps, and filed past the principal. He watched us march back in the school.

"Wait," he said, and motioned to me. This was it. I'd risked it all and for what? Nothing had changed. But then no one demanded anything. No one yelled; no tear gas was thrown. I'd sat on the grass for twenty minutes, missing class, for nothing. And now, I was about to lose my cheerleader status.

"You've got grass sticking to your skirt," Mr. Henson pointed out.

"What? I do? Oh, thanks." I scurried into the school, swiping my behind of loose grass. I went to Mrs. Deskins's biology class, where most of my classmates were already seated.

No one said a word. Mrs. Deskins got up and approached the blackboard and began talking about mercury, the element, not the planet, I was disappointed to learn.

I also learned stating your rights, and fighting for them against injustice, was exhilarating. I was eager for the next protest.

# CHAPTER 21

# THE NERVOUS HOSPITAL

MOM FOLDED TOWELS, WARM FROM the dryer. Towels, washcloths, hand towels, all folded with edges perfectly matched. She patted the final towel on the stack, turned, and walked out the door. Mom went down the four steps from the porch, stepped into the yard and out onto the road in front of our home. She turned left and walked, head up, wringing her hands, crying.

When our next-door neighbor, Mae, looked up from sweeping her porch, she saw Mom stepping resolutely along the road, staring ahead; Mae noticed Mom's shoulders shaking from crying. She called to her. "Jean! Jean! Where are you going? What's wrong?" Mom sobbed that she was going to her sister's house in Milton, ten miles away.

Mae threw down her broom and raced inside her house. She called my Aunt Norma. Norma got in her car, driving toward our house. She found Mom walking beside the road. Mom got in Norma's car, and she took her to her home. She called Dad when she knew he'd be home from work. He drove to Norma's to pick up Mom.

When I came home from high school, the house was empty. Dad had taken Mom to the local hospital, where she was evaluated and then committed to the State Mental Hospital in

Huntington, about twenty-five miles away. I have no recollection of Dad's return.

I thought all this happening meant Mom would leave Dad again, but I had no idea where we would go. We lived near Norma now, which Mom had wanted for a long time. I didn't know what was going to happen. No one told me anything.

****

Mom often said her mother, whom I never met because she'd died nine years before I was born, predicted what each of her children would be like when they grew up. She said my mother would be a one-man woman. She would never leave whoever it was she married. I guess it was the truth because after a few tries, she always came back.

My grandmother died when Mom was ten. Mom's father, for reasons no one told me, or would tell me, sent his five youngest children, Mom and four of her sisters, to live with his oldest son, Herman. Herman, sixteen years older than Mom, was married to a woman who everyone called Old Ruth, who beat and berated Mom and her sisters nonstop, so they each eventually told me. The older girls escaped by quitting school, getting jobs, or marrying and moving away.

My aunt Norma recalled to me the day she and Mom moved out of Herman's house. She said that Mom was sick. "Jean had a felon, an abscess of the bone, in one finger. It throbbed and ached, and she cried and cried. Old Ruth decided Jean should wash dishes. Jean wailed she couldn't, that she was in too much pain. It was awful. I took up for Jean, and Old Ruth began to beat me." My aunt shook her head and paused at the memory.

"As sick as Jean was," my aunt continued, "she stood up and pushed her away from me. Old Ruth went into a rage. She started beating Jean. I ran down to our brother Kenny's house and told him what was happening. He came and got me and Jean and took us to a house he owned and was going to rent. We started living in Kenny's rental house. I was fourteen and your mom was sixteen. Old Ruth was furious and stalked us, waited for us outside the house, threatening to kill us if she caught us."

Mom missed the entire ninth grade when she became ill with a kidney disease. The school arranged for lessons to be sent to her at home, but I always thought maybe she fell too far behind in her schoolwork. She quit school in the tenth grade and went to work in a dime store. Life was good for a couple years, especially as they had a safe place to live. Then she met Dad. The jokes and laughter between them came easily. He seemed solid, secure. He smiled at her, and she was lost in his good looks.

****

After Mom was committed to the State Mental Hospital, Dad and I drove thirty minutes to see her a day or two later. I don't remember the drive, but memory returns with the images I saw once we reached Mom's floor. Dad and I got off the elevator and stepped through two open doors into what looked like a lounge. To one end was a large television with couches flanking it, and a huge, oblong coffee table between. On either couch, men and women were sitting in their pajamas staring at the television. I assumed they were patients, like Mom. A nurse's station was to our left with two women in white uniforms. Next to the station was a door with a small window. I was tall enough to see in the room, but all it contained was a gurney with straps dangling from its sides.

A nurse approached Dad. They spoke, and then she disappeared into a room off to the right. The nurse soon returned, leading Mom, who was dressed in a long, flannel nightgown. Her usually neat blonde hair was awry, her face red and swollen. She clasped and unclasped her raw, chapped hands. As she approached Dad, I hung back, but I saw her put her hand on the back of her head. I heard her say, "A man hit me on the head with the cue stick. It bled." I looked toward the pool table at the back of the room.

A male patient in a rage had hit her. "They put him in there," she said, pointing to the room with the gurney and straps. I don't remember if she spoke directly to me. Dad led Mom back into the room where she had come from, and I stood and watched the other unmoving patients rapt in front of the television.

I didn't know they were going to give Mom electroshock therapy, and if I had, I wouldn't have understood.

*****

On the drive home from the hospital, I noticed the late fall sky: clear, turning purple and soft. I hunkered down on the passenger seat. Dad said nothing, and I didn't know what to say. My memories swirled around one another, and I thought about the night when I was eight, and the visitor came to my room and wrapped her arms around me, the night when Dad threw up blood in Mom's sink. The way I had come to think of it was it might have been an angel who came to me. Whatever it was, I needed that warmth then. I cheered myself up: I would be all right. Remember? None of this will happen to me.

I said nothing to Dad or anyone else, but I wondered when Mom would come home.

I was old enough to see Mom as more than a cook or house cleaner, who fussed about my behavior. She had a fantastic sense of humor, a trademark talent to mimic people, and she startled everyone regularly with her sharp wit.

Her brother, Kenny, was a lay minister. She often mimicked the man, who spoke in a whisper to his congregation. The whisper was a result of his experience in World War II, when his ship was blown out from under him, and he floated in the ocean for twenty-four hours before being rescued. She mimicked him out of love, not to make fun of him, but he was fair game. Everyone was.

"Well," she'd whisper, "I faced the congregation, and I told them how they'd better live at the foot of the cross lest they find themselves in a lake of fire!" She thumped her hand on a book on her footstool and stood, finger in the air to deliver a perfect oration of her brother.

"I tell you brothers and sisters, it weren't but a few days ago I set myself on fire. Yes, that's right. I was burning brush, and the wind changed. Now, you know don't you, the winds of life can change. You're fine one minute, raking up brush, doing what you're supposed to do, then the next minute, your britches are on fire, and your wife is fussing at you, hollering, 'Keeeennnnny! Your pants are smolderin'!' I tell you brothers and sisters, they's nothing worse than coming home with your pants a-smoldering and your wife ready to hit you with her broom!"

Years later, when the movie *Sling Blade* came out, about commitment to a mental hospital, Mom would imitate actor Billy Bob Thornton's character in the movie. She'd growl, "They sent me to the Nervous Hospital." We all laughed, which was always her intention, to laugh when she could about anything serious. It kept her "feet on the ground and head out of the clouds," she'd say.

While she often mimicked many folks, she also had a beautiful alto voice, and when she was young, she'd sung duets in church with her sister, Norma, or often the two of them formed quartets with young men in the church. They were invited to sing at other churches all around the region.

I remember many times when I was small, sitting on the porch on a warm summer night, hearing Mom and Norma sing old hymns, sounding like angels, tapping toes in time with the melody. They raptured me straight to heaven with their beautiful harmony.

When Mom wasn't sitting around making us laugh, she loved to go to yard sales. Norma always drove, as Mom never would drive. She eventually got her driver's license, but Dad always told her she wasn't capable, that she'd wreck and kill people. Ironically, he seemed to have forgotten that's exactly what he did back when I was little. He hadn't killed the man, but he put him in the hospital when their cars collided head on. It took him ten years to pay the man's hospital bill, and Dad's license was suspended. He was only allowed to drive to work and back, but he always went anywhere he wanted.

When I was old enough to get my driver's license, she and I hit the neighborhoods on the weekends in search of bargains, or rather she did. As a teen, I wasn't much interested in bric-a-brac and old curtains, but I never minded taking her. Or she hit the yard sales with Norma. Otherwise, she rarely got out of the house, except to the grocery store with Dad.

A good yard sale to Mom was when she found a stash of used paperbacks and good, barely used clothes. She was a voracious reader. We'd return home, and she'd gather her sacks around her, digging down into them and hauling out her finds, deciding whether she'd keep her treasures or pass anything on.

"I think this blouse would fit Wanda. She's bigger in the bust than I am. I know Ruth hasn't read this novel. I'll let her have it first. I bought this little ceramic pitcher for you. It's blue and white. Your favorite colors."

****

Sometimes, Dad would come home from a beer joint and go get his hunting rifle, load it. He was going to kill a person for an imagined slight. Mom wrestled the gun away on more than one occasion. If she was lucky, she'd convince him to stay home and eat. She knew that if he'd eat, he'd soon get sleepy enough to go to bed. Always the next morning, no sight of the gun, no word of the fight. At those times, we looked like an ordinary working-class family.

One time when I was about fourteen, I was sitting on the floor under the Christmas tree. Mom was on the couch, and we were talking about the presents. The door burst open, and Dad staggered in. He careened toward me, then tottered, about to fall on me. I reached up, put my hand against his chest and shoved him back hard. Regaining his balance, he staggered back. I saw his fist curl, ready to hit. Mom leapt off the couch and over the coffee table; like an unmovable statue, she stood between me and Dad. She stared at him, her hand raised. He stepped back, uncurled his fist, then stood for a moment with his head down.

No word passed between them, and he turned and went down the hall to their bedroom. Mom relaxed her stance. As she sat down and lit a cigarette, she put her finger on her temple, resting her head against it, her elbow on her chair arm. She sighed. Smoke exhaled with the sighs, turning the room a hazy blue.

We never talked at these times. The incident lay between us, raw like red meat. Words came later when she told her sister about it. She and I had a silence between us, unspoken feelings. It had always been that way. I never asked, I never complained. It would have added to her grief. Maybe add to her anger, which I hated to risk.

****

A long time ago, when Dad turned thirteen, his father told him to get in the truck, they were going to Big Earl's. When they arrived, his father said, "Set him up! Whiskey!" Dad began his own journey like his father's—the stumbling joyride of drinking men. My grandfather clapped my dad's thin back after he'd downed a shot of whiskey, and bellowed, "Now, you're a man!" It was a tradition, the same ritual my grandfather went through with his uncles. Neither man had a chance. Neither man overcame the desire for drink. It was a desire stronger than anything else.

****

One day Mom was at the sink washing dishes, staring out the window, waiting for Dad to come home. He'd been drunk for several days, wandering in and out of the house, driving her insane, she said. I was silently finishing my homework at the dinner table. I saw her shoulders lift and felt myself holding my breath. Here it came. The sigh. I slammed my pencil down. "Stop it! Stop sighing!" I burst out.

She whirled around, shock on her face, "What are you talking about?"

"Don't you know? Don't you realize you sigh constantly?" I thumped my fist on the kitchen table. Then I could feel my face aflame; I immediately felt the shame, but I said nothing else.

My anger spent, fear took its place.

I had never talked to my mother that way. I never even thought to do so. My mind boggled with bad thoughts of my mother's disappointment in me; my body slumped from exhaustion.

I had spent all of my life drowning in her sighs. Drowning in Dad's whiskey, though I had never taken a drink.

She stared at me a few seconds, her mouth hanging open, then turned back to the pot she was washing. "I didn't know it bothered you," was all she said.

\*\*\*\*

When Mom underwent electroshock therapy, it was 1969. She said she remembered being strapped down on a table. They placed a chunk of hard rubber in her mouth. Nurses on either side of her grabbed her arms and legs. Something similar to headphones were placed on her head, a rectangular pad above each ear. They told her to hold still and then she remembers falling, falling, falling . . .

I only visited Mom one other time in the mental hospital. She had begun the shock therapy, Dad had told me. But this time we went into her room. She was in bed, one of four in the room. I stood at the foot of hers watching her. Her eyes darted about the room as if they had a mind of their own. She fidgeted with an energy she barely contained. Her hands crumpled a tissue over and over. Upon noticing us, she cried, "I want to go home." Dad shook his head and told her she had to stay a bit longer.

"It was horrible," she spit out through clenched teeth. "The electric shocks. It felt like I was falling . . ."

What fell now were her tears, constantly streaming down her cheeks, soaking the front of her gown, as the tissue in her hand became a wet lump. She snuffled hard, and suddenly looked at me. "Where did you get those pants?" she demanded.

I looked down at my slim, gold-colored jeans. "You gave them to me," I told her.

"I don't remember them," she said, shaking her head. I didn't know it then, but electroshock therapy can have a major side effect: memory loss. So I was stunned. Why wouldn't Mom remember the the pants I was wearing had been hers?

Suddenly her attention diverted to a bed across the room. She pointed to a woman lying motionless. "No one comes to check on her. I check her breathing once in a while. She's been like that for days." The woman's head was completely swathed in bandages, with only a small gap over her nose. I tiptoed over to see if she was breathing but detected no movement. I turned to speak, but Mom was sobbing again.

I watched Mom from across the room. She was speaking to Dad, but it was as if the sound was turned off. I thought about how I had kissed her soft cheek each morning of my life before I left for school. Her blue eyes, I always thought the color of cornflowers, now seemed grey, like the color of cold rain. She looked so tiny in the bed.

**\*\*\*\***

Mom came home on Christmas Eve. The day before, Dad let me have the car, and asked me to shop for a Christmas present for Mom. I had no idea what to buy with the thirty dollars he gave me. I bought a navy blue suit at a dress shop. Mom never wore it. It was years before I learned that the suit I'd bought was almost identical to the one she wore when she married Dad.

It was already dark when Dad returned with her and her suitcase, which he took straight to their bedroom. Mom remained in the living room. I was on the couch, pretending an interest in a television show. I had no idea what to say. I never said welcome home, how are you, nothing. I couldn't seem to move toward her, to hug her, to kiss her cheek. She never spoke to me, asked me how I'd been. We both stared at the television.

When Dad returned from the bedroom, she rose and came toward him. She embraced him, something I'd never seen her do in front of me. They were directly in my view, blocking the television. Dad's arms were locked rigid at his sides. She looked at him, into his eyes. "I love you, Vernon." Her voice cracked and she seemed ready to cry. He hesitated then chuckled, "Well . . . I love you too." He stepped back and patted her on the arm and asked her if she was hungry. He hurried toward the kitchen. Her head dropped, and she stared at the floor; I saw her back expand, heard the air hiss into her lungs. She folded her hands over her stomach as she let out a long sigh. "No. I'm not hungry," she said.

**\*\*\*\***

Psychiatrist's Clinical Notes          1970

Name: Doris J.

Age: 34

Sex: F

Married: Husband, George V.

Occ: Kaiser Alum. Date: 12-14-69

First Year

14 Jan. 70 — Pt. first time post hospital. Depressed, crying. Not considering suicide. Husband drinking excessively. Staying at sister's. Husband not considerate. Pt. has flu. Elavil 50 t i d.

9 Feb. 70 — Pt. at home. "I'm not myself." Sleep, timid feeling, crying improved. Elavil 25 t i d.

20 Mar. 70 — Feeling fear or dread of recurring depression. Denies suicidal thoughts.

20 Apr. 70 — Pt's husband cut back at work. Unable to pay bill. Still depressed—cut back on meds due to financial pressures. No tears shed at father's funeral. He had been a Hell fire and brimstone preacher. Mean. Afraid of him.

8 June 70 — Fearful of return to hospital and further ECT's. Serax 15 t. i. d.

20 July 70 — Lessened fatigue, feeling of dread. Likes to laugh and joke. Childhood not happy. Grade school above average student. Lots of friends.

30 Nov. 70 — Nervous as Christmas gets closer. Has had illness at or near Christmas for several years. Apprehensive—fears going back to hospital.

****

YOU LIVE WITH IT, WITH many things, and you don't know what to call it. You can't see the larger picture; all you can see are the small details that don't seem to add up to anything you can grasp. We all accepted that she'd be fine after her ordeal. We didn't even question the wisdom of the medication when she fell once again into a deep depression when he was drunk or when she anticipated he would be.

The doctors told Mom she'd forget all sorts of information that was easily retrieved before. She might not remember moments of her childhood and her focus and concentration might deteriorate. The point of the treatment was to forget, hopefully not the sweet memories of her life, or the practical data we all remember, but she would forget what it was that was making her so sad. They put her on Elavil, a medication for a chemical imbalance of the brain. No one ever mentioned, nor did it occur to me until long years later, that she never seemed depressed when my father was sober.

It didn't seem to me memory lapse was ever a great problem for Mom. She never spoke of the loss as the years passed, except to mention older childhood memories she couldn't remember.

To me, she had the sharpest memory of anyone I've ever known. Her stories of being young, being with her family, then her marriage, when my dad would leave and not return, she'd tell me these stories over and over. The same each time, as if reciting poetry or the ballads of the bards. "Write them," she'd tell me time and again. "Write my story so people will know what it was like."

**\*\*\*\***

### Psychiatrist's Notes—First Decade

4 Jan. 71 – Got through Christmas by working every day. Aventyl 25 mg # 42 desp.

13 Oct. 71 – Enjoying work. Having migraines.

29 Nov. 71 – Having all kinds of crazy spells, feels dizzy. Senequan 25 t. i. d. q. i. d. Taking Premarin.

12 Aug. 72 – Had single 2 week period of depression in last 4 months.

10 Jan. 73 – Did well at Christmas. Fearful of driving car. Cont. senequan.

4 Feb. 75 – Laid off work. Depressed.

20 Aug. 75 – Pt. has learned to sew—unable to charge for work yet.

15 Aug. 77 – Bouts of depression. Husband drinks more when she works. Says, "It's his problem."

15 Feb. 78 – Child gone. Husband drinking more, missing work. Depressed.

16 Feb. 79 – Husband still drinking in binges.

14 Aug. 79 – Husband still drinking.


Psychiatrist's Notes—Next Decade

25 Jan. 83 – Has gained some weight. Complaining of dread.

27 Mar. 84 – Has had flu. Great interest in grandchild. No bouts of depression.

26 June 84 – Pt.'s brother recently deceased. Mourning appropriate.

29 Jan. 85 – Pt. concerned for granddaughter heart surgery. Husband charged with DWI.

7 June 85 – G. child doing well. Husband drinking less. Cont. meds.

3 June 86 – Husband still drinking. She's writing a book.

1 Mar. 88 – Husband drinking more.

24 Jan. 89 – Husband decides to retire. Daughter moves to Texas.

12 June 90 – Husband stops drinking 6 months. Sister moves to S. Carolina. Traumatic separation. Ludiomil cont.

2 June 92 – Pt. moving to S. Carolina. Mood improved.

Notes from family doctor:

Mrs. Hodges has been treated by Dr. —— for 23 years. Transfer records to Dr. —— in S. Carolina.

*****

# CHAPTER 22

# MY KINGDOM FOR A HORSE

"I DON'T READ THOSE," MY mother snorted, referring to the paperback book she had in her hand. "If it has a car in it, it's too modern for me to read." She dropped it back in a paper bag at her feet and continued browsing through the selection my Aunt Wanda had brought on her previous visit. "Most of these are romances." She studied the title and wrinkled her nose.

Tossing that one back in the bag, she hauled another out and after a quick glance, tossed it my way, shaking her head. I picked it up and looked at the cover and saw an artist's rendering of a bare-chested man, with a rippling six-pack abdomen, pulling a half-dressed woman to him.

"I thought you liked bodice rippers, Mom. At least that's what they seem to be when you look at all the book covers."

"No sir. Can't abide them." She smoothed her blonde hair and adjusted her oversized reading glasses. "Oh, look here. Here's one that should be good." She was studying a book titled *Kentucky Hills*. On the cover was a woman about to be ravished by a man dressed in buckskins. Apparently it wasn't a bodice ripper if it took place in the distant American past, and the man and woman were in remnants of pioneer apparel.

"This takes place in the late 1700s. They're pushing into Kentucky." She studied the plot summary on the back of the book. "Says here they're living in a sod house. I don't think so. Not in Kentucky! Sod houses were out in the prairies!"

\*\*\*\*

One of my most vivid images of Mom is of her seated in her chair, table lamp glowing in broad daylight, absorbed in a book. Mornings, she was up at 5 a.m., and the house was spotless by 9 a.m. Then she was free for the rest of the day to read. Reading time was interrupted only by a twice-a-day phone conversation with my Aunt Norma. At 4 p.m., she began cooking supper, even though she and my dad didn't eat until 5:30.

"I like the food to simble," she said, mimicking my grandmother's misuse of the word for simmer. Mom cooked dinner slowly, because in between pot lid lifting and taste testing, she'd read a few more pages. Over the years, she'd passed through phases of reading particular kinds of books. I first noticed what she read in the late sixties, when all the books were about slavery. For months she'd spout, "Naw saw, massah," in answer to a question.

"My God, what they went through, those slaves. It was horrible!" her constant lament during this reading phase. "I wish they all could have gotten away from those plantation owners." Mom remained indignant about this American injustice and spoke of it often.

Then in the late seventies, she read nothing but books about American Indians and for a long time would say, "If it can go wrong, old Whatashie here will get blamed for it," as she pointed to her own chest. Whatashie was apparently a name she picked up from a novel about American Indians. Once again she became indignant. "My grandmother was a Cherokee. Lord, no wonder she was in a nasty mood all the time."

After that, pioneer books became her mainstay. I owe my considerable knowledge of pioneer life to her. Two of her favorite books were Alexander Thom's *Follow the River* and Janice Holt Giles's *Hannah Fowler*. I held the latter up one day, noting it had no colorful dust jacket. "What's this about?" I asked her. She took the book from me and studied it. "You should read this. It's one about the old days. It was incredible."

"What do you mean?"

"The pioneers were moving west into Kentucky. Proud, strong people. They had it so hard. Hannah Fowler reminds me of my own mother and grandmother. Neither ever had much, but they made it." She darted her blue eyes in my direction to see if I was listening. "You could learn a lot from reading my books, you know." Her books, she called them, as if they were personal friends. Often she'd read to me passages of language that were beautiful in imagery or funny or informative. Always, a book lay near, pages marked, ready to receive her into its world again.

I learned colorful words from her reading. Mom's speech remained chock-full of pioneer dialect, in which she ruled as an expert, by her own calculation. "Whar you a-goin?" "I'm gonna kill me a bahr for supper." "Hit'll do, I reckon."

Her language skills didn't stop with books. She created words and their meaning. "You needn't do that; it ain't compulsorary." Compulsorary meant, I think, an action that seemed compulsory to do but a person is too contrary to actually do it, so it was okay if you didn't.

Or she'd insist: "Put the Kyustus on that!" Meaning, quietus.

If it could be said simply, in Standard English, she'd rather not. "Where's the fun in that?" she used to ask me, or anyone else who commented on her dialectal habits.

"One thing your mother liked in school was reading," my aunt Norma told me. "Hated math, but she'd read anything, even Shakespeare."

"I don't remember there being any Shakespeare around the house growing up," I noted.

"No. I guess not. We read it in school. I suppose that's where she got it from, those phrases she used to say."

"Like 'my kingdom for a horse'?"

"Yeah, or variations of it, among others. Lots of phrases from the Bible, too. We were reared in a church. I guess she likes to liven up her speech."

When I was small, she read to me all the time. I have misty memories of sitting beside her, nestled against her body, my small hand on her arm as she turned the pages of a children's book. I listened to her read, her voice resonant and soothing, as images played out in my mind of cats chasing leaves and dogs fetching sticks. A nosey blonde girl bothered three bears, and a wolf ate a little girl who wore a red hood. When I was older, she told me about the day I came home and showed her I had learned to read. I was five and in the first grade. She said I burst in to our apartment and pulled her from the kitchen interrupting her cooking. I made her sit beside me; I opened a book and read *Dick and Jane* to her. She was astounded. "One day you couldn't read," she said, "and it seemed the next you could, as if by magic."

\*\*\*\*

I looked at my mother, studying another pioneer novel she'd pulled from the paper bag like a jewel from a treasure chest. I knew she wondered if it would be a good read, a good story, factual and delightful, heartbreaking and inspirational. Just one word after another marching across the page, carrying my mother to an uncomplicated, understandable universe, where it did not matter what happened to slaves or American Indians or pioneers because the author would see that justice, love, and good will would triumph, not like real life.

Mom's intention for me to read and understand *Hannah Fowler* seemed to be that Hannah was a role model of a strong, independent woman, willing to take on challenges and win with humility and gratitude.

I never told my mother that it was she who stood as a role model for me.

# CHAPTER 23

# NIGHT ON CHEAT MOUNTAIN, PART 1

GRANDFATHER, 1950

"We'd been back on Cheat Mountain deer hunting. Been up there all weekend. We came down on Sunday.

"Vernon, me and him'd been hunting. We didn't get nothing. I think Harry got one, didn't he, Vern? Yeah, I think he did.

"We was coming down off the mountain. It was darker than pitch. Cold too. I came around one of those curves, and I guess Vern rolled out on the other side. Damned door had come loose when we rolled it in the river that night.

"Well, damned if it wasn't a little bit before I knew he wasn't in the Jeep! He rolled out of it. Went over the side. Hell, I had to turn around and go clear back up on the mountain. There he was, standing there beside the road.

"Anyway, I stopped and picked him up, and we turned around and came on home."

****

FATHER, 1975

"We'd gone back up on Cheat Mountain to deer hunt. Well, I didn't get no deer. Neither did Dad. We decided to come on home.

"We ran into Russell, and Lord he was drunk. We got to rac-
ing. I was driving the Jeep, and next thing I know, damned if
we didn't miss a curve and run the Jeep straight into the river.
Well, hell, it wasn't deep. It'd been pretty dry all summer.

"Well, anyhow, we got 'er straightened up, and I guess we
musta busted the door on the passenger side. Dad drove then.
You know how them mountain roads are, I mean straight up
and down and with them kiss-your-ass turns. Anyway, we was
coming down, and I guess Dad took a sharp turn to the left and
that busted door came right open and out I rolled."

"It was the damnedest thing . . ."

# CHAPTER 24

# NIGHT ON CHEAT MOUNTAIN, PART 2

DAUGHTER, 2015

The hunting party had been small: my grandfather, my father, a few other male relatives. Uncle Red got a big buck that my grandfather had flushed toward him in the grey dawn light. The kill freshly gutted, my grandfather and my father decided to head back to the camp. Each man's breath steamed the air as he walked to the small cinder-block, one-room building, with an outhouse behind it. They hand pumped water into a big pan, water for coffee in the morning, for rinsing a glass to refill with whiskey or beer.

These two and a couple others, with no more kill to gut, spent the day drinking Old Crow, which was all they had left, and about dark, my grandfather and father decided to go home. My father drove first, and my grandfather nodded drowsily on the passenger's side. But then my grandfather's cousin Russell followed him from the camp and pulled his truck beside their Jeep. He leaned out in the darkening, cold air and shouted to my father, "Hey Vern! You think that piece of junk can beat my truck?" He grinned, saluted, and the race was on.

Down the mountain they sped, often side by side. Coming around a sharp curve, just before climbing another steep hill on Cheat Mountain, my father overshot the turn, and the Jeep rattled down a small bank and whammed onto its side in the Cheat River.

Father and son climbed out and studied the situation. Wasn't nothing to do but push the Jeep upright in the river. Luckily, the water was low, hardly over their ankles, but rocky and slippery. It took the better part of an hour, but the three men managed to right the Jeep, drive it back up the small bank and onto the road.

This time, my grandfather drove. They saluted Russell, who sped down the road ahead of them, the victor. My grandfather had a loose grip on the steering wheel and almost dozed, the sound of pumpkin-ball bullets rolling on the floor-boards as he wove around curves, up and down the mountain. He day-dreamed and maybe sleep-dreamed of Wild Turkey and Old Crow. My father had fallen asleep and leaned against the pas-senger door. My grandfather, drowsy and warm in the truck, came into a kiss-your-ass turn and startled at the suddenness of the bank coming up he was about to overshoot, he jerked the steering wheel to the left, struggling to keep the Jeep on the road.

"Damn!" he muttered, as he fought the steering wheel. My father, asleep against the damaged passenger door, suddenly found himself airborne, as the door had flung open in the sharp turn. He sailed out over the embankment, landing about a third of the way down, where he tumbled over and over to the bot-tom. He slammed up against a few small trees, then lay on his back, stunned.

His breathing was labored because he'd had the wind knocked out of him, but in a few seconds, he inhaled and then slowed his heart to nearer normal. The night was inky black, with no sounds. In October in the mountains, the tree peepers have begun to hibernate, and the crickets have given up the ghost. He rolled over on his back, assessing the damage—was anything numb? Could he move his limbs? Now, he was beginning to feel the cold as he stared at the star-filled night sky. Not only were the animals silent, he realized, but he didn't hear the sound of the Jeep, either.

He sighed and sat up. His elbows and knees stung from scraping gravel on this tumble down the embankment. *Damn,* he thought. *If I hadn't been drunk, this would've killed me.* How far had he rolled? He looked up toward the road. In the faintest of light coming from the west, he could see the top of the bank at the edge of the road. No father, no other car engines.

My grandfather had continued driving down the mountain, unaware his son had flown out the door and down a hill. The door swung back, latching loosely, when he came out of the sharp curve and swayed in the opposite direction. On down the snaky road a bit, he decided he wanted a cigarette. He reached in his shirt pocket and pulled out a crumpled—and empty— cigarette pack.

My father struggled up the embankment to the road side, grabbing a shrub he'd encountered in the almost complete darkness. When he stood upright at the side of the road, he was winded again. He listened, and sure enough, here came the grumbling sounds of the low-geared Jeep, back up the mountain.

"Dad must need a cigarette," he mumbled to himself. He stood, nursing a now aching knee, hobbling around a bit, making sure most things worked okay. Then the headlights of the

Jeep appeared down the hill from him. Dad watched as the Jeep swung around a curve, momentarily disappearing, then come back into view as it swung toward him at last.

The headlights bathed my father in bright light. His father U-turned the Jeep in the narrow road, teasing the steep embankment on the other side with the Jeep. But at the last minute, he backed it up, rocked it around, and was headed, once more, toward home.

"Damn, Dad. I rolled clear down the bank," my father laughed as he hung onto the open door of the Jeep. "Didn't you even know I was gone?"

"Not till I needed a cigarette." My grandfather harrumphed. My father climbed into the Jeep, pulling the passenger door shut with both hands. It wouldn't stay all the way shut, but he'd just have to stay awake till the road straightened out. That would be another fifteen miles anyway.

They both laughed and joked about Dad rolling out of the Jeep as they drove on down Cheat Mountain and back home.

It was a good story to tell, which they did, over and over through the years.

# CHAPTER 25

# CarnieVAL

"WHERE ARE YOU GOING?" MOM asked as she dusted the table beside her chair. Her cigarette ashes had blown out of the ashtray. This was a woman who made my bed—still—two minutes after I got out of it. At least she never complained I didn't make my bed. I never had the chance.

"To the carnival." I took my wallet out to see if I had any money—only one dollar. "Do you have any money?"

She straightened from her task, giving the table a final flick. "I have a five. That's all that's left from the grocery money your dad gave me. Will that do?"

"Yeah. Valerie said she didn't need gas money. So that will buy me enough ride tickets."

"Well, your dad will give me more money Friday, when he gets paid. That is if he goes to work."

"Where is he this time?"

"God only knows. He told me he was going fishing with Zeph up in the mountains, and he'd be back tonight. I'll believe it when I see it. Probably sitting down at Kings Drive Inn."

After fishing in her purse, she opened her wallet and handed me the five.

I heard a car horn. "There's Valerie."

"Don't be in here late."

Valerie's Ford Fairlane purred down Route 60, windows open, the wind whipping our hair, stinging our cheeks. Her car was ugly—beat-up and scarred, but I marveled that she even had a car of her own. I only got to drive Mom to the store and to her psychiatrist in Dad's Plymouth Valiant.

We talked about school and boys. Eventually, talk turned to her mother. Then about her mostly absent father.

"At least you have one. You might not know where he is all the time, but you have one who comes home occasionally."

"Sometimes sober. Sometimes not," I reminded her.

"But he's home most of the time. And you have a mother who worries about where you are." Valerie slowed down the car and pulled into a field now being used as a parking lot.

"Your mom seems nice. Mine—she makes my bed and won't let me cook."

"Gee. That's terrible!" Valerie moved to get her purse in the backseat.

"Okay, smart-ass. I get it."

"Do you?" Valerie turned off the motor and turned to me. "You don't know how lucky you are."

She opened the door and swung out, slamming it behind her. She leaned in the window. "What are you waiting for? An invitation? Let's go CARNIVAL!"

We bought ride tickets at a booth and slipped into the throng of people. Cotton candy and popcorn smells assailed our noses. Games of all sorts gave carnival-goers the chance to win massive stuffed animals. Toss the ring. Shoot the ducks. Have your weight and age guessed.

We rode the tilt-a-whirl, then the merry-go-round. The little kids' roller coaster gave me a headache, but it eased up on the Ferris wheel. The night air was soft, and a full moon lit up the fairway. Valerie and I were stopped at the top as others climbed on the ride.

"Hey! You notice those two guys?"

I looked over the bar of the seat. The only two guys close to the Ferris wheel were the ones who put us on the ride. They looked to be about our age or maybe a couple years older. One was operating the ride; the other helped riders get on and off the cars.

"They work here," I said as I leaned back against the seat.

"So? What's your point? They're cute."

"They're carnies."

"I'm surprised you know that word." Valerie turned to me and grinned. "Maybe you're not as naïve as I thought."

"Oh, you think I'm naïve, do you?" I asked just as the wheel began moving again. Each time we passed the carnies, Valerie waved and hollered, "Hey cuties!" When we got off the ride, Valerie approached the taller and slightly beefier of the two. I hung back, not sure where this was going. He laughed with her, and the other one looked at me. I smiled and waved, but I didn't come closer. I noticed, though, the one looking at me was quite cute. He vaguely looked like Paul McCartney.

Valerie came over to me and linked arms. "Come on, Miss Innocent Pie. We got us a couple dates!" She pulled me toward the two. Getting closer, I saw that they were indeed older.

"This one," Valerie pointed toward the beefier one, "is Sam. And this one, is Paul."

"Paul?" She had to be kidding. The one who looked like Paul

McCartney was named Paul. Now that I was standing next to him, I noticed in the bright lights his eyes were blue.

"Hey, ladies. Your luck is about to change!" Sam's fist pumped the air. "It's the end of our shift!" A couple other carnies walked up. Sam and Paul talked with them briefly, then turned to us.

"Let's treat the ladies to beer, Sam. What's your name?" Paul asked me, turning to walk beside me as we made our way toward the edge of the carnival. I looked around for a stand selling beer and saw none. "My name is Cat."

"Cat? Okay then, Cat. What do you do?"

"I'm in the eleventh grade."

Paul stopped in his tracks. "Wait! Sam! We have a couple young ones here."

Sam turned to look at Paul, but didn't break stride. "So? What's your point, man?"

Paul hesitated then put his hand around my upper arm. We strode a little faster to catch up with Valerie and Sam. Now, we were beyond the carnival and out of the lights. Up ahead, just a few yards, was a motel. The parking-lot lights and the moon illuminated its shabbiness. Trash littered the pavement.

"Where are we going? Where's this beer? I thought it was in a stand at the carnival."

At my side, Paul didn't look at me as he answered. "Sam and I have beer in our room. Eleventh grade, huh? What do you like most about school?"

"School? English, I guess. I like to write. I like history and gym."

"Gym? Are you one of those athletic types? Brainy, too. How about that?"

Up ahead, Sam and Valerie had reached a motel door. Sam fished in his pocket for a key. The door swung open, and he and Valerie stepped inside into the dark.

I hesitated and looked at Paul. He laughed. "It's okay. You'll be okay."

I stepped into the room as Sam turned on the light between two twin beds. Valerie immediately fell onto her back on the bed. Sam fell on top of her and they "went to town" as my mother would say as she watched a sexy scene on television.

I looked up at Paul and noticed in the lamp light his pupils were huge, allowing for little blue to show. "Wanna beer?" He moved toward a cooler on the floor by the dresser. Valerie and Sam were making smacking noises and rubbing each other, grabbing body parts. Sweat formed under my hair and at the top of my lip.

Paul pulled me over to the other bed and we sat down. He handed me a beer, then took it back to pop the cap off with a bottle opener. He pointed with his own beer to Sam and Valerie. "She seems pretty used to this."

"Valerie? I don't know . . ." I watched her and Sam. Now, he had his hand down her shorts. I turned my head, trying to think fast. *How was I going to get out of here?* I looked at the door.

Paul touched my arm. "So, you study English and history?"

I looked at him, again noticing his beautiful blue eyes with the large pupils. Now that I paid closer attention, he didn't look like Paul McCartney after all. Only his hair was a Beatle cut. He smelled like sweat.

"Yeah, I guess so. What do you like about school?"

Paul laughed. "Oh, I've been out of school a long time. Quit when I was 12. Joined the carnival route. I liked math, though. I might have stayed if my old man hadn't beat up my mom and my sister and throwed me out of the house when I fought him back. I liked history too. Can't say I liked English, though. Too hard."

Before I could answer, Sam reached up and turned off the lamp. I peered through the dimness to where the moon shone in the window by the door. I panicked, my body tensing.

Paul sat quietly, drinking his beer. My eyes adjusted to the dark. I started to tell Paul I wanted to go, but he leaned in toward me to kiss me. It was oddly sweet, just a pressing of lips, no pressure at all. I pulled back, saying nothing. Again, my mind was blank. I heard moaning noises coming from Valerie and Sam.

"You want out of here, don't you, Miss English?"

"Yes," I whispered. I couldn't see Paul's eyes. He was a dark shape beside me. The beer in my hand was cold and sweaty. I swallowed and looked toward the window where the parking-lot lights shone through dimly. Suddenly, Paul stood up and pulled me up off the bed.

"Okay, Cat. Out you go!" We strode over to the door, and Paul jerked it open. He put his hand in the small of my back and shoved me slightly. He plucked the beer from my hand.

"But Valerie! She has to come with me." I turned toward the room again.

"Don't worry about her. She and Sam will be fine." He closed the door in my face. I stood staring at its peeling paint, studying the peep hole, wondering if I could see in the room as well as out. I pounded on the door, and I swallowed over and over, my mouth dry. Paul jerked it open.

I stammered, "Valerie has to come with me." Behind Paul, Valerie spoke. "You go on back to the carnival. I'll be out in a while. I'll give you a ride home. Don't worry about it."

"Valerie, you should come out." I stood stock-still, trying to see into the dark room. Paul tipped up his beer bottle and drank deeply.

"Get out, kid. I'll be fine." *What was she doing calling me kid?* Paul shrugged and shut the door again.

I turned and walked back to the carnival, staring at the bright lights, debating what to do. I wandered from game to game, idly watching people lose dimes, lose dollars. As I approached the tilt-a-whirl, I saw a couple students I knew from a nearby high school. I walked to the ride and waited for them.

"Hey, Cat! How'd you get here?" Did everyone know I had no car?

"I came with Valerie."

"Where is she?" June asked, looking into the crowd.

"Oh, around." *Why was I staying silent? Why didn't I get them to go back to the room and help me get Valerie out?*

The one named Sandy laughed, "I'm surprised you're with her. She's a slut. She's probably over in that hotel screwing a carnie."

I was shocked. How did she know Valerie? We went to different schools, and I knew the two of them vaguely through cheerleading years ago. Did they see the two of us go to the motel? "She's not a slut." I said.

June nudged Sandy. "Come on, Sandy. You don't know those rumors are true."

They linked arms and moved away from me, June saying, "We're going on the Rocket. Wanna come on the ride with us?"

The Rocket was the one ride I always avoided. It consisted of two cages, one on either end of a long arm. It spun, making you think you'd be slammed into the ground at any moment.

Like a robot, I followed them. They were at least people I knew. Sort of. I looked around, noticing the bright lights, the cheap stuffed animals, the drunken riders, the girls with shorts too short, with boobs bobbing as they laughed up into a guy's face. Little kids dragged parents from one ride to the next.

We had arrived at the Rocket. I handed over a ticket and stepped into a cage, expecting Sandy and June to follow, but the carnie shut the door. "Sorry," he said. "There are three of you and only two to a cage." The ride moved my cage up into the air, where he then helped Sandy and June into the second cage. I looked out from that height. The moon reflected off the river. A few boats sent ripples out. I heard the roar of laughter from the carnival goers, the calliope music from the merry-go-round. I looked over to the right and saw the motel, with its dirty parking lot. I gripped the bar in front of me.

The cage suddenly plummeted toward the earth. Almost before I realized what was happening, I was swept within inches of the ground, my head seemingly about to be smashed into bits. Then I swung upward again. I faced the night sky, the stars barely visible beyond the carnival lights. Then just as fast, the cage plummeted down toward the ground again, but it swiveled so that I was free-falling backward. My heart pounded loudly in my ears, and I gripped the bar in front of me so tightly my hands ached. Once again, I was flung past certain death and up toward the sky. For a second I was weightless. Then back down again, this time forward. I screamed.

I was still screaming when the carnie opened my cage door. "Hey, little lady. The ride's over. You're safe." I opened my eyes, staring forward, and clamped my mouth shut. *Was it possible? I survived?*

As I shakily stepped out of the cage of death, as I thought of it, I saw June and Sandy move off to another ride. I looked in the direction of the motel. It had been so long. I had to get Valerie out . . . somehow.

But there she stood, near the darts booth, smiling and alone.

"Valerie!" I shouted her name as I ran toward her. I stopped short of her.

"Are you okay?" I was panting.

"Sure. What'd you think?"

"I thought I wouldn't see you again."

She snorted. "I'm fine."

"What happened?"

She shook her head. "Did you know Sam is twenty-three?"

"No. But I figured they were older than us. Eighteen maybe."

"He's twenty-three, and Paul is twenty-one. They've both been on the road with the carnival since they were kids."

"Paul told me. He was twelve. His dad beat up his mom and sister. His dad threw him out when he tried to protect them."

"Is that what he told you?"

"Yeah. What'd he tell you?"

She grabbed my arm and pulled me along. "Come on. Let's get home."

"What'd he tell you?"

She stopped and looked at me closely. In the carnival's bright lights, I saw her eyes were dilated. "There's dads, and then there's dads. I think you're lucky to have the one you have."

"He drinks. Right now, Mom isn't sure where he is." *Where was this conversation going?*

"He comes home, doesn't he? Eventually? You have what you need . . ."

"You have food, clothes. And a car. Well, he's never spanked me. My mom would never let him . . ."

"Yeah." she said, squeezing my arm. She steered me across the highway and into the field where her car was parked. The car's tires burned rubber once we hit the highway. I gripped the edges of my seat and felt slammed against the back of it, just like the Rocket.

Valerie turned up the radio. We couldn't talk over the music. She sang loudly to the Beatles's "Helter Skelter."

When we got to my house, she turned the radio down. She looked at me and smiled. "Here you are, home. Safe and sound." I put my hand on the door handle, turning to her. "You sure you're okay? You shouldn't have stayed in that room. With Sam. They were men . . ."

"It took *you* a while to figure that out, didn't it?"

I hesitated. She was right. I hadn't protested but followed as if it was all okay. Paul had let me go.

"See you at school on Monday." She put the car in reverse.

"Right. You read your history chapter?" I opened my door and stepped out, turning to hear what she'd say.

"Yeah, yeah. See you, Cat."

As Valerie backed out of my driveway and turned the car around, I saw one taillight was out. I'd have to remember to tell her so the cops wouldn't stop her and give her a ticket.

In the morning, I got up out of bed and headed to the bathroom. I came out and glanced in my room. My bed was made, the surface smooth, taut enough to bounce a dime on. Mom was back in the kitchen making breakfast. The smell of bacon filled the room. Dad, who had come home from the mountains, was sitting at the table reading the newspaper. A breeze ruffled Mom's white curtains over the sink.

I sat down to eggs and bacon. I told Mom I'd ridden the

Rocket, that I had thought I was going to die. I told her I'd never do that again. Ever. She nodded, saying those things were dangerous and should be outlawed. People go to a carnival to have fun, not be scared to death or be afraid they were going to die.

I had seconds on the bacon. I looked up to see the sun shining through the window and on the counter, gleaming off the silverware, casting a bright and glittering light.

# CHAPTER 26

# WAR

A PILE OF RUBBLE *rose to at least fifteen feet, stretching down the middle of the avenue. Smoke obliterated the sight of buildings in the distance, leaving only those flanking the rubble in detail. The windows of the buildings lining the street were dark, glass broken. A few buildings were destroyed completely. An acrid stench, like petroleum or heavy metals, filled the air, and I put my hand over my mouth as I climbed to the top. I began walking the rubble's length, stumbling as broken bricks turned over. Before me lay an unending line of debris marching on until it disappeared into the fog and smoke.*

*No other human or animal was about. I peered into empty building windows. No one. Sunshine barely penetrated the thick air. I coughed, looked down at my hand to see spots of blood. I wiped the blood on my pants and looked up to the right. One building had a steel door on the front with a metal handle. I stopped and stared at it, then felt compelled to open it. I scrambled down off the pile, bricks falling behind me, hitting my legs and back. I approached the door. It gleamed as if in a noonday sun, but I could not see where the light was coming from. My breathing shallowed to short puffs.*

*I reached for the handle and clasped it firmly, willing myself to yank it toward me. But it gave easily, almost knocking me down. I released the handle, and the door swung open. Inside*

*was a small room, and in the middle was a pile of dead people,
all stacked like cordwood up into the sky. No roof, no boundary.
Just dead people piled up and up and up. I knew then the world
had come to an end.*

Dream, age fifteen.

****

Boy #1

When the school bus dropped me off in front of my home, I
immediately saw him leaning against the maple tree in the side
yard. His left foot was propped up against the tree, and his back
was against the trunk. I recognized him as a guy I had met at
the city-hall dances. I walked toward him, curious as to why he
was in my yard.

"Hi! What are you doing here?" I asked as I came closer to
him. He was short, I thought. Just barely taller than I was, but
I liked his blond hair. It was cropped close but lay in coarse
waves. He was in shadow, but I could see his eyes were green.
At the dances, I had danced with him a few times, but in the
strobing lights in the darkened hall, I couldn't tell much about
his features.

"I came to see you. Your mom said you'd be home soon."

"You're out of school, aren't you? Did you graduate?"

"No. Dropped out of Winfield last year." He shifted his foot
off the tree and turned toward me. He rested his shoulder
against the bark.

"I got called up."

"Called up? You mean drafted?"

"Yeah. I leave in the morning for boot camp."

I didn't know what to say. He took two coins out of his

pocket and rubbed them together between thumb and fore-finger.

His head jerked up, and in a breath he rushed out: "Will you write to me?"

"Sure! I'd be happy to. Do you have my address? You can write to me when you get where you're going . . . Do you think they'll send you to Vietnam?"

He continued rubbing the coins, but faster.

"Why wouldn't they?"

****

Boy #2

A red car roared into our short driveway. I came to the door, anxious for my mother to not see this one. He was short, too, with dark hair, older than I was by three years. It was a couple months after the first one was in my yard, leaning against our maple tree. This one shoved open the driver's side door and yelled: "Like this? You wanna drive it?" I had a learner's permit.

"Yeah! You bet!" I hoped my mother didn't hear that exchange. I turned back into the house long enough to tell Mom my date was outside. She yelled for me to be home at 9 p.m. I'd just gotten the privilege to go on car dates. I rushed down our porch steps and to the passenger side door. "Better wait till we're on the road before I drive."

A block away I was behind the wheel of a sleek red Buick. The interior was white leather. I turned off our block and onto the main road. It was sweet, cruising along the road.

"Drive over to the school yard. I want to show you something."

The school was a couple miles away. We chatted, and I was

curious. I pulled onto the empty school lot. He leaned toward me and kissed me.

He got out of the car and motioned for me to join him. He walked over to a patch of grass to a flagpole. He stopped at the pole and looked up. The American flag lay limp, no breeze encouraging it to unfurl.

"I'm going in the Marines. I'll be going to Vietnam, probably." He kept looking up. I looked up, too, not sure where all this was going. He put his arm around my shoulder and pointed up. "Ain't she beautiful?"

"I guess so."

We stood for a few more moments. "When I come back, will you marry me?"

I leaned away from him. He didn't look at me, just up, at the flag. "Marry you? I hardly know you." I laughed, thinking he was joking. He tightened his grip on my shoulder, pulling me to him again.

"I'll give you the Buick. And buy you a house."

"Well . . . thanks. But I don't think so." I felt his arm grow tighter. Now it was getting uncomfortable. "Um, maybe we should go. Want to go to the Dairy Queen for a shake?"

He pounded his fist a couple times against my arm, but he let me go. "Sure you won't change your mind? You'd have it nice, I guarantee."

"Thanks, but . . . I'm only fifteen."

He turned to face me quickly. "Oh, if that's all you're worried about, I'll be in the Marines four years and when I get out you'll be nineteen."

The next day, I refused to take his many calls. He stopped calling on the second night.

## Boy #3

I was never in school with the next one. He graduated before I stepped into high school the first time. But I had seen him in town, at the dances, and with other people I knew. He was gorgeous, blonde hair, with a sweet smile. He wasn't really funny, but I made him laugh with my goofiness. When I saw him at the dances, I had hoped he'd ask me to dance. Finally, he did, and we danced on a hot summer night till we were both soaked with sweat. We went outside the city hall so he could smoke. We sat on a low wall and talked quietly for nearly an hour.

After that, we dated every weekend. We went to movies, more dances, out to eat at Pizza Hut and the Dairy Queen. He bought me a cake for my sixteenth birthday. We swam, picnicked, and kissed every chance we got. Then we couldn't get enough of each other. The passion grew and grew. I thought of him constantly and even felt that in the future we would marry. He showed up for a date one cool, fall evening to tell me he'd scored a low number on the draft lottery. He was fast-tracked to boot camp. I could barely breathe whenever I thought about it. "Don't wait for me," he said. I nodded, numb. "Okay, if you say so."

****

Months went by, and I didn't hear from this last boy, the only one I wanted to hear from. I listened to my mother and father fight. I barely noticed when my father came in late or not at all. My mother seemed to float through the house, but I'd been witness for too many years.

I ran around with girlfriends, ones who had cars. I met other guys and then other guys and then other guys. Later, a few went off to war, but by that time, I was no longer dating them, or we'd had only one date.

As my future loomed, I had no idea what I would do when I finished high school, which I was due to accomplish shortly. I had dreams of what I might do, but they seemed unreal, too impossible for me to try to make them come true. My parents said they would pay for college, but I seemed to be waiting. For what, I didn't know.

****

SOLDIER #1

He came back from the jungle, I heard. He had been a tail gunner on a helicopter. A bullet ripped through the copter floor and on through his foot, so they sent him home. I never saw him after he was in my yard, leaning against our tree. He never wrote to me from Vietnam.

****

SOLDIER #2

He did come home from the Marines four years later. He married and bought his bride a house and a car. I heard he had the largest American flag in the state on a huge flagpole in his yard.

****

SOLDIER #3

When he returned, he called me. I waited by the back door, watching for him. I was excited, nervous. It had been two years since I'd seen him. I never heard from him during the war. I wrote letters to him that I never mailed because I had no address for him. In those unsent letters, I told him what I was doing—girl stuff: who's dating whom, the dresses I wore, how I had cut my hair again. Occasionally, I wrote about the rising anger by some Americans for American soldiers. I thought these angry Americans were mad at the wrong people. It was the government they should be angry with, not the soldiers. Even after I read about My Lai.

I wondered if it would be like it had been before between the two of us. I never really expected, though I had hoped, I'd at least see him again. He was my first real love, and here he was back. My head buzzed with the possibilities for the future.

When he came to pick me up, I clung to his arm as he drove. I chatted nonstop, about family, school, mutual friends. He was quiet, nodding, and smiling, new lines crinkled around his blue eyes.

We parked in an old parking spot. It was his turn to talk, and he talked about Vietnam: the battles and slogging through the jungle, about the Viet Cong. Then he told me about how soldiers kill the enemy, civilians, anything and anyone. His attitude was matter of fact, as if he'd gone to the grocery store for the last year and a half and had just returned.

"I saw people on the news marching against the war. They were saying our soldiers were participating in a bad war . . ." I paused, unsure of where my comment was going. But I plunged ahead. "I am not against the soldiers, but it seemed as if many are killing for the sake of killing . . ." I got no further.

"What do any of you know about war? What do *you* know about what it's like? To be over there, to come back and feel betrayed and spit on and damned because we're over there doing what we're supposed to be doing! You are stupid if you think it's all that easy. You don't understand anything."

I was shocked into silence. I reached for him, but he pulled away. Further attempts at talking, cajoling him into listening to me, to talk to me failed. In silence, he drove me home. I stepped out of the car, and he slammed it into gear and roared in reverse, jerking it to a stop and then raced forward on the road. I stood until I no longer saw the taillights. I stayed outside by the road crying. I don't know how long. I was just glad my parents were in bed when I came in. I didn't want them to see my face.

I never saw him again.

****

One evening after dinner, a few days after soldier number three left me beside the road, I decided to watch the late news on television. I don't remember who the reporter was, but then I saw a soldier running through the jungle. Suddenly, he was shot, a chunk of flesh flying from his chest. Boom! Down he goes. I sat stunned, wondering if what I saw was real.

If my mother wondered why I was so silent in recent days, I wouldn't have told her, but she never asked. Guilt began to eat at me for being so ignorant and so stupid, to be so foolish as to not understand anything at all about war. I watched television and saw the riots, saw people who looked normal and sane spit on our returning soldiers. I was disgusted, but over and over I thought, *How am I any different?*

We had no idea what it was like to be in a jungle, to hump pound upon pound of ammunition and weapons and rations. Suffer foot rot and napalm. Helicopters resounding in your dreams: *whump, whump, whump.* Family so far away, almost dim in your memory. Ugliness and pain, drug-addled gunfire, tunnels to death.

****

Graduation came, and afterward, I was hired as a waitress at a diner, my future still unclear. Then one night the dream returned, and once again the world was devastated. I came down off the rubble and stopped in front of the shiny metal door; it came open easily.

Behind it lay soldiers, dozens and dozens of them, piled up into the sky.

# CHAPTER 27

# THE SAILOR MAN

"I'm supposed to meet Larry at 9 p.m. He won't get off work till then," I told my friend Terry. We were parked at Shoney's, where they still offered curb service. It wasn't unusual to meet friends and then hop in one another's cars to run around, find a place to park, and smoke pot—if we had any.

A car parked next to us, and we nodded hello to the guys inside. Terry knew one of them but not the other. After talking back and forth over the lit menu boards, one of them, Dan, got in our car for a ride around the area. He had pot. We didn't.

I decided he was cute. Cute enough to kiss, so I did. When we arrived back at Shoney's, we continued to talk. Wasn't he surprised when Larry's car drove up, and I hopped out for my date?

The next day, I borrowed my dad's car and drove to Dan's house. It's a wonder he would even speak to me, but I had decided he was the one.

Dan was five years older than I and had spent four years in the Navy during the Vietnam War. We talked long hours about his time on the USS *Forestall*, about tending the boilers that ran the ship. But there was no talk about Vietnam, the jungle. I discovered our attitudes were the same about war and pretty much everything else. To my surprise, this man listened to me. I realized that my intuition, that he was the one, was right. We married eight months after our first date.

There was no test I had to pass—about war, killing, soldiers. He didn't think I was naïve and dumb. And maybe, after what had happened with soldier number three, I was no longer naïve, even though I was only nineteen.

Soldier number two had been correct: at nineteen, I would marry. Just not him.

I left my parents' home to make my own. At last, I breathed.

LOSS . . .

# CHAPTER 28

# IN THE CELLAR

IN THE CELLAR, WHERE SPIDERS as big as my hand lived in dark, dank corners, I kicked at paper bags full of empty pints of Old Crow and Wild Turkey. Jim Beam lingered in one bottle, and I dribbled him out in my hand—a pale, brown liquid that streamed to the concrete floor and puddled.

The whiskey's acrid smell lingered in my nose as I considered the life represented by these overflowing, paper grocery bags full of bottles, now emptied of their promise.

My grandmother hovered at the door, her slender frame a silhouette, the only accent a little pooched-out belly. She nodded toward the bags, as she stepped back out into the light.

"These ten bags are a month's supply of whiskey, all watered down to make it last," she said.

She flicked ashes from the end of her cigarette and sighed.

"He's so far gone, he don't know."

# CHAPTER 29

# RECKONING

When I was in my early twenties, I had not been to see my grandparents for many months. I arrived on a dog-day afternoon in July. My grandfather, if not at the end of the table in the kitchen, spent his days on the front porch. He watched the occasional car go by, stirring up a dust cloud, and smoked his cigarettes. He swayed to and fro in the swing all afternoon.

When I arrived that sweltering day, I had parked my car beside the front porch and walked around to the steps because I had glimpsed Poppaw in the swing. I had just stepped up on the porch when he suddenly jolted to half-standing and drew back his fist.

"What the hell you doin' here?" he screamed at me. Startled, I stepped back down a step, not sure what to do. "Dammit! Get back to Kentucky where you belong!" He shook his fist and then plopped back onto the swing. I noticed my grandmother standing in the doorway behind the screen.

"He thinks you're somebody from back in Kentucky come to try to kill him."

I was stunned. What on earth was she talking about? I'd never heard this story. I turned to look at Poppaw, and he'd settled back down in his swing, smoking, looking out beyond the banisters to nothing.

My grandmother came out of the house and sat down in a green metal lawn chair. I came cautiously over to another green chair and sat down, watching my grandfather warily.

"One day, not too long ago," she said, "the telephone man stepped up on the porch to deliver a phone book, I reckon. He didn't see Warren at first. Then Warren yelled, 'You'll not get me! It was self-defense.'" My grandmother chuckled, stopped, and lit a cigarette.

"I reckon Warren scared that phone man to death. He turned and ran off the porch and back to his truck. I don't think the telephone man'll be back again.

"His mind's gone," she told me, drawing on her cigarette. "He thinks everyone who steps on this porch is from a long time ago, and they want him dead after all these years. When he was over in Kentucky laying gas lines for the company, he got into messes." She blew cigarette smoke out her nose and shook her head.

I watched him. His hands were huge and puffy, swollen so much his fingers seemed to fuse into massive blobs. His arms, exposed where his shirtsleeves were rolled back, were covered in open sores. His cheek jowls quivered whenever he moved his head. His hair, now white, was still as curly as ever. He seemed much older than sixty-eight.

My grandmother, in contrast, was wearing a fresh white blouse, her red shorts sharply creased. Her hair, softly permed and tinted blue, flattered her prominent cheekbones as her best feature. From my position, I watched her face and wondered how she'd coped with my grandfather all those years. She pointed to him, but looked out through the vines for a glimpse of the road. "They say the mind goes before the body in people who drink like he does. I 'spect that's a race in his case, which'll go first." She looked back at my grandfather, inhaled deeply on her cigarette, and blew smoke toward him. He swatted at it as if flies buzzed his head.

# CHAPTER 30

# EXCEPTION TO THE RULE

It was odd, but stories about my grandfather getting into messes in Kentucky were not stories repeated within the family, that I know. My grandmother only mentioned it one time and never said exactly what had happened. My father told me that most men back in the wilds of Kentucky during the twenties and thirties carried a gun. And they didn't hesitate to use them. I suspected my father knew a great deal more than he was telling me.

Bits and pieces of stories about Kentucky floated around the edge of my consciousness, as if hidden behind thick curtains.

Even within a family of storytellers, a few get away. You have to let them go and leave them in the past, untold, unknown, a secret carried to the grave.

# CHAPTER 31

# CHARMED

"You'd better not go see him, Cat."

"Why not, Dad?"

"Well . . . he doesn't look like himself. He's all bloated up . . . I'd rather you not go see him. Your mom's there, helping out. Mom's there too."

"Have they said whether he'll come out of the hospital or not?"

"No. Your grandfather's not going to come out, Cat . . ."

"Oh. Okay."

****

At the funeral, I was cloistered in a side room with my family while the visitors filed into the funeral home. I looked over at my grandmother, tears flowing down her cheeks, a hanky held to her nose, but she said nothing. *I cannot imagine,* I thought, *what she's thinking after forty-six years of marriage. What hopes and dreams did she harbor as a young woman?* I recalled my favorite photo: him in jodhpurs and a low-slung driving cap, cigarette hanging from his lip. Her—so young—with dark, wedge- cut hair, Mary Jane shoes, and a little slip of a dress that fell to her knees. Her arm resting across his shoulder, looking toward him.

At least, I'd always thought she was looking toward him, but I was unsure; maybe she was looking past him. I'd have to look at the photo again. I'd thought of them in that photo as James Dean—the Wild One—and her, next to him, waiting for excitement. Well, she got plenty, but whether or not it was what she really wanted, I don't know. By the time I came along, her first girl grandchild, the third grandchild, she was a typical grandmother. Home was her center: canning, cooking, cleaning.

When the folding wall that had partitioned the family was moved aside, we were exposed to the attendees like contestants on a game show or a jury in a courtroom. My eyes found my grandfather. He lay in an open casket. They'd put a brown suit on him.

The preacher gave a credible talk about my grandfather, reminding the audience of his achievement as a welder, that he was legendary. "Why, men came from far away to watch Warren weld. He was one of the first to successfully try an experimental weld on a live gas line. Others had tried it and been blown up for their troubles."

An accolade. An accomplishment to be proud of. Men—from all around—came to see him weld.

"Mom," I asked after the funeral, "what was Poppaw like when he was in the hospital?"

"When he went in, he mostly didn't know anyone by that time," she said. "The doctor said his organs had shut down. At the end, I was dabbing at his forehead with a wet washcloth. I was wearing a charm bracelet. He reached up with his index finger and started tinkling the charms together. We didn't think he knew any of us was around. I took my arm away, and he lowered his hand. When I went to wipe his forehead again, he reached up and played with the charms again. He had a smile on his face. I guess the noise got through, and he liked it. It seemed like he was a kid playing with a toy."

****

*"Punkin, want to go with me to feed the hogs?"*

*"I sure do, Poppaw." I hung onto his beefy index finger that filled up my small hand. He wiggled out of my grasp to ruffle my hair and smile down at me. He laughed and walked and walked and walked until he was out of my sight, a big figure of a man, with translucent blue eyes that never faded.*

# CHAPTER 32

# I'VE DRAWN UP A MITE

When I came into the hospital room, an orderly was hoisting my grandmother up from her bed in a sling that had a scale attached. "I'm weighing your grandmother," he said to me. "We need to know her weight so we can judge medicine amounts."

Slowly, he lowered her back to the bed and deftly slid the sling from under her. He leaned over to my grandmother, who was on her side. "How tall are you, Ma'am?"

"Well, I used to be five foot five, but I suspect I've drawn up a mite."

To this day, whenever a comment comes up about how tall one of us are, my husband and I always finish with, "But I suspect I've drawn up a mite." It always gets a laugh.

Nearly twenty years after my grandfather died, my grandmother, by then eighty-three, was in the hospital, and it did not look good. No one really knew exactly what was wrong with her, other than she had smoked for sixty-five years. A blockage of blood to her legs seemed to be the main problem, probably veins that had narrowed due to all the smoking. Test after test didn't show anything conclusive. After the first week in the hospital, she stopped talking. She seemed to be sleeping much of the time, and when she roused, she moaned in pain. The moans became louder and louder, often becoming near-screams as the weeks went by. Then they increased her morphine, and she stopped. A few times she called out, "Mommy!"

Her mother had died when my grandmother was a teenager. My father had told me the story: Ann Nelson's youngest child, Chester, was about two and ill. Chester was my grandmother's youngest sibling. Ann climbed the stairs to the bedroom to check on him. At the top of the stairs sat a chest with blankets. She retrieved an extra blanket for her son, but when she stepped back, she stepped too far and tumbled backward down the steps. The doctor came, but he said she was "all busted up inside." Nothing would help. She lingered nine days, then died.

****

For six weeks, my grandmother remained in the hospital. I came to stay with Mommaw day after day and on a couple nights, propping myself between two chairs to sleep. I was in school, about to finish my bachelor's degree in English and taking care of my husband and young daughter. Other relatives, her siblings and grandchildren, came to see her, standing about the room, talking to one another, as Mommaw was unresponsive.

It was a vigil, I understood. She wasn't going to come back from this. Still, it was a shock when I came one morning about 10 a.m. and stepped into the doorway of my grandmother's room. I stopped abruptly. The bed was empty.

A nurse nearby saw me and came over to me. "I'm sorry honey, didn't anyone tell you? Your grandmother passed away early this morning."

I'm sure my mouth hung open. I knew it was coming, but everyone's always surprised when it happens. I looked back at the sterile room, the bed neatly made, waiting for the next occupant.

My world shrank a bit more.

# CHAPTER 33

# 900 DEGREES CELSIUS

CRUCIBLE

My dad and I sat in plastic scoop chairs in the surgery center's waiting room. He was to have his carotid artery unclogged. I had traveled to South Carolina, where my parents had retired. Mom, as always, wanted to be near my aunt Norma, who had moved south a few years before. Now, Mom was undergoing chemotherapy and was in another hospital across town to have her port changed, through which she received medicine. I came to be with Dad during his surgery.

The waiting room was full, and a television mounted near the ceiling blared a *Jerry Springer* show. The show's guests were screaming at one another and occasionally baring gums where teeth should be. I tried not to glance up at the television too often. Dad stared straight ahead at a small child with a gauze patch over his eye, who stared back at Dad with his good eye.

Shifting in the uncomfortable plastic chair, I knew I'd never sat this close to Dad. Our thighs almost touched. When I was still at home, he always sat at one end of the table, with me at the other, and Mom in between.

Dad didn't appear nervous about his upcoming surgery and didn't seem inclined to talk. Silence, if you could call it that with the television blare, yawned between Dad and me. Given that we rarely had lengthy conversations, and I didn't recall ever asking him questions, I had no idea what possessed me to suddenly ask: "Dad, what was it like working at Kaiser Aluminum? How's aluminum made?" He'd retired seven years earlier after working in the finishing mill for decades. In that part of the plant, he inspected thin sheets of aluminum that would be made into foil and beer cans. Still, I knew little about what he did and nothing about the aluminum-making process.

"Well," he launched as if he'd been anticipating the questions, "aluminum comes from bauxite. It's mined in different places in the world—Africa is one place. They dig it up and then crush it to help remove other minerals. They wash the bauxite, sort it by size, then separate the liquids and solids to remove clay, mostly. It's a slurry then, you see, sort of like a soup. They take that slurry and dissolve it in fluoride compounds, put an electric current through the bath, then you get alumina."

"Alumina?" I interrupted. "Not aluminum?"

"Yeah, the ore at that point is called alumina. You don't get aluminum until you mix it with carbon dioxide. They put it into a smelter, and the carbon dioxide evaporates, and you're left with aluminum."

Dad paused in his story when the gauzed-eye boy walked over to him, reached out, and touched his knee. The boy's mother called him back, explaining, "He thinks you have gum in your pocket."

Dad reached up to his shirt pocket and rummaged around, but I knew he never chewed gum.

"Well there partner, I seem to be plum out of gum. But here," he reached into his pants pocket, "here's a dime."

Without a word, the boy took the dime, glancing back at his mother, who nodded. Then he slipped back to his mother and took up staring at Dad again.

"Anyhow," he turned to me, "they'd ship the aluminum to our plants then. You remember that piece of bauxite I gave you?"

"Yeah, I still have it in my cedar chest. It's silver."

"That's right. And it never tarnished, did it?"

"No, it's just as silver and shiny as the day you gave it to me." I must have been eight years old or so, nearly thirty-eight years ago.

"Aluminum forms from alumina at 900 degrees Celsius, but once the aluminum is formed, it melts at 660 degrees Celsius. At the plant, they smelt it with other metals in huge metal pots—they're called crucibles—that can hold hundreds of pounds of smelted ore swinging from massive cranes overhead in the pot room. Cranes lift two huge, oblong, molten ingots I always thought looked like the Devil's shoes passing over us."

I interrupted again. "I thought you never worked in the pot rooms?"

"Well, I went in from time to time, needing to talk about the slabs of metal coming to us in the finishing end that had flaws. We'd talk to the pot room guys, see if they knew what the problem was. I tell you," he shook his head and tsked, "I don't know how they stood it. The temperatures in the pot rooms reach 180 degrees Fahrenheit at a man's shoulder. You know your Uncle Jack worked in the pot rooms his whole time at the plant. I suspect that's why he can't breathe well now. The lines are wrapped in asbestos, like this . . ." His hand made a wrapping motion around the opposite arm as if he were swathing a wound.

"I've seen the men in those rooms look as if they'd been working underground in a coal mine, their faces were so black. They wear this heat-protective garb that looks like big yellow raincoats. If they didn't wear them, they'd burn. You know those huge pots can never be turned off. Once they're heated, it takes massive amounts of energy to reheat them if they ever get cool. It looks like the furnaces of hell. Sparks fly, men up on catwalks get covered in sparks, but they just keep moving, using these big cant hooks to tip the crucibles, and out pours molten metal. It goes into molds to make the ingots."

His hands gestured in grand arcs as he described the pot room. When he told of the crucibles tipping, his hands looked as if they held a large pot.

"It takes a special kind of person to be able to work in those pot rooms. In my end of the plant, the rolling mills were pretty tame. They pour the alloy into huge rectangular molds, making slabs of metal a couple feet thick. These slabs go through huge, heavy rollers and get pressed into metal for car bumpers or beer cans or aluminum foil. We had it easy on that end. But not the pot room guys. They could do things I never could."

BENEFICIATION

"I forgot to tell you they do a thing called beneficiation early on with the ore. They upgrade the ore this way, mix it with other metals. I guess you can't just work with what you get out of the ground, and once you dig it up, it's quite a process, you know, to get it to where it's aluminum. And it takes so much gas to fire those pot rooms—it costs around three million dollars a month to keep those pot lines fired up."

A nurse appeared at the door of the waiting room and called

my father's name, interrupting his story. It was then I noticed about half the former *Jerry Springer* watchers were looking at Dad, obviously listening.

"Yeah!" Dad answered and stood up.

"Come with me, sir. You can come, too," she pointed to me with her pen. We followed her to another room where Dad answered a series of questions about who was going to pay what insurance didn't cover, whether he smoked, was he retired. I sat quietly, still thinking about the aluminum plant, seeing in my mind's eye the smelting pots and the Devil's shoes.

I'd always thought my facility and love of language came from my mom, who was an avid reader and ached to be a writer. Dad was also a voracious reader. I have a love of reading thanks to both of them. Yet, I conceded that Dad was a good storyteller, which is a skill most of my family members had honed all their lives. The high adventures Dad participated in as a young man, and even as a retired older man, seemed natural for storytelling. He told stories of his youth often. Work, now that I thought about it, he had rarely talked about. It was what he had to do. He did tell stories about the people he worked with, usually a funny story.

I remembered my mom's comments that in the early eighties he'd been trained on new equipment and handled it all so well the company had flown him from the Ohio Valley to California and Canada to train others. His ease in understanding machinery, woodworking, tool use, and mechanics was astounding. Over the years, he'd disassembled cars and trucks down to the chassis and rebuilt them. My mom often found a weird-looking tool he had fashioned to do a particular job.

Another nurse came to fetch Dad after he'd told his personal business to the billing department woman. Again, I was told to come along. I was beginning to wonder if I were going into surgery with him.

This nurse took Dad's blood pressure, temperature, and respiration. He was asked to put on a hospital gown, and when he came out of the bathroom, he was told to get in bed. Once again, he had to answer questions.

"Do you smoke?"

"No. I used to. Quit several years ago."

"Do you drink, sir?"

"Oh, once in a while." The nurse looked at me and winked.

"Well, that's good. Too much drink harms your health." Apparently she knew from his blood work he'd been on a bender recently. I managed to not look directly at Dad.


Rolling, Rolling, Rolling

The nurse finished asking Dad questions, and we were left alone. Silence again stretched between us. He fiddled with the bed covers, moved items on his tray—the water pitcher, a box of tissues, straws. I'd brought papers from my freshman composition class to grade, so I took them out of my satchel and began reading. I'd just begun teaching full-time.

"Well," he suddenly spoke, startling me, "the ingots we got into our rolling mills are a little over two feet thick, about twenty feet long." He measured about two feet with his hands. "The slabs can weigh twenty tons." He looked from his hands up to me. His eyebrows rose, which I remembered was his way of checking if his audience was listening. The brows lowered. "Those slabs are heated in a furnace and rolled between powered rollers until the ingot—then it was called a plate—is pressed to about an inch thick." He measured the one inch between thumb and forefinger. "Then that's when I got 'em. They come to my finishing mill and we hot rolled them to about the thickness of a quarter of an inch." The space between his thumb and forefinger narrowed. "I was one of the inspectors. If it didn't suit me, then I rejected it."

The door opened to his room, and an orderly came in with a gurney, followed by two nurses. They helped Dad onto the gurney and with a nurse on each side, pushed him through the door and turned left down a long corridor. I followed along, chatting with the nurses and noticed Dad began to look a bit anxious. The doctor who'd performed the catheterization the week before was disturbed by how clogged the carotid artery appeared to be. He told Dad that he had a 50 percent chance of suffering a stroke after the surgery. He added that he would do his best to keep that from happening.

They rolled him the length of the corridor and stopped short of double doors. One nurse turned to smile at me and told me where I could go to wait until after Dad's surgery.

The doors swung open automatically, and the surgery unit lay ahead. Dad didn't look back at me but raised his left arm, index finger in the air. It was a wave so-long. Then he was through the doors and out of my sight.

I headed for the hospital's cafeteria to get something to eat and to call my mom with an update. She was exhausted, she told me, and was going to try to nap. But I was to call her as soon as Dad came out of surgery.

Although it was January, no one had removed the Christmas decorations. I waited for the cooks to load my tray with something resembling meatloaf and stared at a happy snowman decoration. Up near the ceiling, tired-looking red garland dangled in several places. Near the elevator, an artificial tree with red bulbs gently vibrated to the breeze of the elevator doors opening and closing.

I thought about how all my childhood Dad drank heavily at Christmas. I scooped fake mashed potatoes around my metal tray and remembered when I was around eight and noticed our family wasn't quite the Cleaver or Nelson families, who gathered together to sing "Oh Holy Night" and "It Came Upon a Midnight Clear." It was odd to think that tree made of aluminum was now a hot ticket in antique stores.

I remembered how that year, I cared little for the presents piled under the tree. I had absorbed my mom's tension about Dad's behavior. I recognized in an eight-year-old way things really weren't too good in my household. But that's as far as the thought went. I was powerless to make the grown-ups in my life change. Dad was Dad. Drunk and missing. Mom was Mom. Afraid and worried. I remembered what happened that night, but the memory of the warmth that had swaddled me seemed vague, and I questioned if it had ever really happened. Maybe it was just a little kid's way of making herself feel better. I certainly had the power to do so, had done so many times over the years.

****

Dad had completed his story about aluminum by the time they'd wheeled him down the corridor to surgery. The rest, I knew. Not the dispensing of aluminum to various industries, where other companies took the metal and made everything from car bumpers to toys, but I knew how he behaved on the job. Over the years, as his drinking had increased, the foremen of earlier times protected men like Dad. They may have been irritated he missed work or showed up with a hangover, but he was still one of their more talented workers. His work-related decisions and actions were considered smart and capable. Toward the end of his thirty-three-year career at Kaiser, that protection waned, as it had for his father at United Fuel. My father's employers had not said anything to him about retiring, although he had enough company time for full retirement. When the company's employees went on an eighteen-month strike, and they had to endure the country's first employee lockout, Dad decided to retire. Always a union man, he was not interested in carrying the banner any longer. It was time to go. He was sixty-five.

I finished my artificial meal and decided to go back to the waiting room to wait until Dad's surgery was over. The weather outside was threatening. The television in the cafeteria was set to the Weather Channel, and they were predicting ice storms for the area. I would face that challenge when I had to. I arrived in the waiting room where several other patients' families waited. They were reading or watching the television overhead.

## Congratulations: It's a Beer Can

It seemed I had spent no time back in the waiting room when a nurse appeared and called my name. Had enough time elapsed for Dad to have his surgery? It seemed only an hour or so had passed.

She spoke to me over her shoulder as I followed her, "Your father's in recovery. He did just fine. But an ice storm is coming. The surgeon will be in to check your father soon, but he'd like him to go home before the storm hits; otherwise, he'll be stuck here too long."

I'm thinking, *But lady, the doctor said the first twenty-four hours were crucial. He could have a stroke. By the time I get him home he'll have only been here twelve hours.* Of course, it was probably about insurance and money.

I'd have the chance to speak with the doctor, too, she said, and he'd give me instructions on how to take care of my father.

Dad was in bed and appeared to be asleep when I came into recovery. Other patients were in other beds, a few partially hidden by curtains, others not. Several had family with them; others were being attended by nurses. It seemed a remarkably noisy and bustling place for recovery. Dad opened his eyes as I approached.

"They're throwing me out," he said.

"I know Dad. I just found out. I'll have to call Mom and let her know we'll be home soon." Just then, a thin man resembling Stephen Hawking approached us. It was Dad's surgeon. He looked at Dad's stitched neck.

"I found what I'd feared I would find when I opened his artery." He gestured toward my dad as if he weren't there. "It was pure sludge in there, the walls were very thin. But I think I've got him stitched up securely. You can take him home in a couple hours. We really are trying to get as many out of here as we can before this storm hits. They're predicting it to be deadly."

*Deadly,* I thought. *And what if he has a stroke? Wouldn't the best place for him to be is in a hospital? If it's going to get as bad as you think, then how's an ambulance going to get to him if he strokes out?*

"Dad, how do you feel about going home now?"

"I feel fine. I'll go home."

Before I could argue anymore, the doctor was saying goodbye and to call him if any complications came up. A nurse came forward and gave Dad instructions on how to care for the wound and what symptoms of stroke to be looking for. She left, and Dad lay his head back on the pillow and soon drifted to sleep. I watched him for a minute, noting his chest rising up and down. I pulled a stool on wheels over to sit and wait.

Two hours later, an orderly and I helped Dad out of the wheelchair they'd provided. I'd been allowed to pull the car up near the surgery entrance. I got in with a wave good-bye to the orderly and drove Dad home.

CRUCIBLE

"You wanted a lunch box just like mine when you started your first day of school. It was one of those aluminum hump-back types. You don't remember? Well, you did. You told your mother you wouldn't go to school unless you had a lunch box exactly like mine. Your mom hunted all over town, but she found one. You even wanted a sticker that said Kaiser Aluminum. So I got you one. Your mother told you she'd fixed peanut butter and jelly for both of us. You went off to school with that little aluminum lunch box. It was exactly like mine."

# CHAPTER 34

# TWIN HALOS

I WAS PACKING A SUITCASE. It was 9:37 p.m. on Friday night, October 6, 2000. The phone rang. I heard my husband say hello. I was folding a shirt, holding it tight against my body, folding and refolding the arms. Shaking it out. Refolding.

I heard him coming down the hallway. I raised my eyes from my task, the shirt tucked under my chin. He caught my eye and shook his head. A wail rose in my throat. Like an animal. No human makes such noises. I felt out of my body, looking down upon myself.

\*\*\*\*

In late September, I had been with Mom in South Carolina, visiting her and dad all that week. I had driven the long nine-hundred-mile round-trip four more times since Dad had had his carotid surgery. I knew Mom's clock was ticking down.

On the day before I left, she was in my car, and we were going to my cousin's house to help her with a yard sale. "Does Katie do well in school?" she asked. She was asking about my daughter, her only grandchild. I glanced over at her, but she was staring straight ahead through the windshield. She was wearing her white turban, with a matching white shirt and capris. Even her tennis shoes were white. Mom was always the natty dresser, coordinated even if she were home alone.

"Yes, she does really well in school."

"Well, does she want to go to college?"

"Yes. She's not sure what she wants to be, but she's going to West Virginia University next fall."

"How's her health?"

"Her health? She's fine, Mom. She's just fine."

"I just wanted to know. Is she happy?"

"Happy? Well, yeah, she's happy. She's okay."

We arrived at the yard sale. It was a cool, windy day for so far south. Customers were steady, and my mother ate a large barbeque sandwich. After her second bout with chemo, she was down to ninety pounds; she had almost no appetite. My aunt Norma remarked later how buoyant my mother seemed that day, and that she ate better than she had in months. "It was because you were there," she told me.

During the sale, I quietly approached her with my camera while she finished chatting with a customer. I took her photo, but she seemed not to notice. I had to go back home. That was on Sunday. She died five days later. I had the photos developed a few weeks after her funeral. I braced myself to look at her. She was smiling.

\*\*\*\*

My aunt told me a ring of white circled the faded blue irises of Mom's eyes. "That happened to Lloyd, too," she said, referring to her late husband. "I remember his eyes looking like that. I knew Jean wouldn't be living much longer."

Rings of light. Twin halos. I wasn't there to see it. I was

seven-and-a-half hours away by car when my mother died in an Augusta, Georgia, hospital.

****

At her funeral, the pastor I had contacted turned out to be an old coach of mine when I was a cheerleader in the ninth grade. He remembered me thirty years later. He didn't know my family or my mother. I gave him all the information about her I could think of at the time so he could build a funeral speech. Not expecting to have to do that, my mind went blank, and I only gave him a few facts. The first thing he asked me, however, was if Mom had been saved. I was relieved to be able to say yes for her sake. My mother, at least, would be spared the harangue at her funeral my grandmother—and all of us—endured at hers.

Just before the funeral, I met my aunt Norma in front of Mom's casket. I struggled to remain standing, to not fall to my knees. My aunt was sniffling, crying into her tissue when suddenly she said, "Oh my God. Jean's going to kill us."

"What?" I looked down at my mother. She looked so small.

"You put the wrong wig on her."

"What are you talking about? You told me the one in the box. The other five were loose in the drawer!"

"Well, she must have switched them out, and I didn't know it. It's the wrong wig. When we die, and see her again, she's going to kill us!"

Then we both laughed. *What utter absurdity, but there you have it*, I thought. It was sort of fitting such a thing would happen and that we laughed about it. Mom and Norma over the years were appalled at any number of mix-ups, screw-ups, theirs or others, it didn't matter. It was all fodder for a long laugh, the jokes and snappy one-liners popping out fast.

**** 

"Jean Hodges was a Democrat devoted to seeing Al Gore follow Bill Clinton into the White House. And fortunately, she was a woman who had given up her life to God many years ago." That non sequitur jolted me out of my grief for a brief moment. For a couple minutes more, the minister summed up my mother's life, merely citing the information I had given him on the phone, word for word, and then launched into his proselytizing with vigor.

"Can you count yourself among those who will step onto the golden streets of Heaven?" he demanded of us. "Have you given your life to the Lord Jesus Christ?" he wanted to know. "What have you done to prove yourself worthy of the Kingdom of God?"

But I was thinking: this is the last time I will see my mother. I had been staring at a remote spot above her casket, but then I looked at her face, shrunken from her battle with cancer, and I remembered how soft her cheek was when I kissed it each morning before going to school. I recalled her eyes, cornflower blue, had faded to a soft grey.

I thought of her cleverness with language, a woman who'd had such little formal education. She had dreams of being a teacher or a writer. She wrote poems and had even started a novel set in the early 1830s in Kentucky. Before she died, I was able to tell her I'd been hired full-time to teach college. I know she was pleased, because family reports filtered back to me, how she told any person who set foot in their house or upon their porch: my daughter teaches college.

One of the first things I looked for in her house after she died were her journals. I'd been buying blank books for her off and on for years, encouraging her to collect her family stories and poems. I wanted to pass them to my daughter. "I'm no writer," she'd tell me. "Besides, I've told you my stories. You write them." I told her that I would. All I found in the journal were five poems, three songs, and three and a half pages of a Kentucky novel she had begun. The remainder of the journal pages were blank, like her lifelong dream.

****

The minister's voice rose to a climactic crescendo at the end of his sermon, jolting me back to the present. I placed my hand on my chest, sensing the heaviness I always feel when I think of my mother since her death. Losing her was like losing a child in the sense of lost potential. I imagined had she lived just a few years more, she might have found peace of mind, moments of grace. Times when she wasn't thinking that my father was coming home drunk.

It wasn't that my mother thought that he would ever quit just because they had moved south, but I know she continued to hope he would. By the time of her death, seven years after they had moved, she knew that day would never come. For several months he would stop, and she would enjoy the quiet. If the dry period lasted for a few weeks, her old enthusiasm for life returned. Her sense of humor sharpened and seemed less ironic and dark. Inevitably, my father would fall off the wagon, and her hope dimmed once again. By the time she was diagnosed with lung cancer in 1998, she knew for certain he would never sober permanently. She was right.

In between visits to see my mother during her illness, I called often to see how she was. Once, Dad answered, and he was drunk again. I lost my temper with him, and for the first time in my life, I let him know it: "You need to be sober, Dad. Mom needs you." I heard a strangling noise, a fumbling of the phone. I strained to listen to what was coming at me through the phone line.

Silence. Then another strangled sound. He said, "What I do is none of your business."

When I came to visit the next time, he was drunk again. He came into the kitchen where I was writing on my laptop, preparing my class lessons.

"What do you think you're doing?" he slurred, teetering by the table, hovering over me.

"I'm preparing my lessons to teach. This is my first semester teaching full-time."

"What do you know about teaching?" His voice was filled with disgust.

"Well, I don't know," I sort of chuckled, not sure where this was going. "I guess I've done it part-time. It worked out okay." I was insecure about whether I knew enough to teach, having begun college at the relatively late age of thirty-six. I noticed he seemed to instinctively know my Achilles' heel.

"What makes you think you know enough to teach?"

"I think I'll go sit with Mom out on the porch." I turned off the laptop and left the room. I stepped out on the porch, where my mother was on the swing, watching the birds in the yard. I was startled to realize he had followed me.

"Well? What do you know about any subject?" I suddenly realized this was punishment. He was punishing me for asking him to stay sober. He never mentioned what I'd said to him, but I knew. I fled again, this time over to my aunt's house next door. He didn't follow.

As Mom's illness worsened, their fighting grew more intense, and all the family came to hate that her final days were in turmoil. I came to hate him, because he would be contrary to her as sick as she was. She was amazingly brave with her chemotherapy, loss of hair and appetite, withstanding the barbarous treatments.

Yet, when my father was sober, he stepped up. He'd make trips to the grocery store to try to find food to tempt her to eat. He gave her the insulin shots she needed—the cancer affected her pancreas—and changed her tubing that kept her bile duct open when the tumor blocked it. He was ill-equipped to be a nurse, but he tried his best.

Toward the end of her life, when she knew she had virtually no chance of surviving, she said to me, "You know what this means, don't you? You're stuck with him." She nodded toward my father who was sitting right in front of us. I said, "I know, Mom. I know."

The last time I had visited her, during the time of the yard sale, I stood in awe in their living room and watched them fight like children, back and forth. She screamed at him and called him names, something she had never done in all the years before. He screamed back. None of it made sense. What they'd argue about were small things, petty things. How a procedure was done or not. My head bounced back and forth between them, like watching a tennis match. I am ashamed to say I ached to go back home. Then it was time for me to return. I kissed her cheek. I told her I'd be back next month.

She seemed to barely be aware of me, that I was leaving. I cried all the way home.

My aunt told me that during Mom's final days in the hospital, she ordered the nurses to contact security to keep my father out of the hospital. He had been drunk for days. "I can't even die in peace," she told my aunt. But Dad came the next day with a tremendous hangover and a book. As my mother lay dying, he read without looking up.

****

The hour of her interment had come; we walked up the slight incline toward the mausoleum, and I noticed the trees were just beginning to turn: blotches of red, yellow, rust, and gold. We stood in a line as Mom's casket was passed through to the little chapel inside. She would be placed six feet up on a shelf, necessitating a stepladder to place flowers in her vase. Her view, if she could sit up and look around at the West Virginia hills, is of the woods and dense thickets. Down over the hill from the mausoleum is a pond often visited by a flock of geese and a quacking duck or two. It is not home, of course. I imagine she has that now. Wherever she is, she knows the joy of a peaceful home where she never has to wait for the other shoe to drop.

# CHAPTER 35

# THE PHONE RINGS

At 3:30 pm on Friday, October 17, 2003, my husband and I were in the kitchen preparing to make pear butter. The phone rang, and I answered. The person asked for me. I sighed. I'd signed us up for the do-not-call list, but an occasional telemarketer still called.

"Yes, this is she."

"Ma'am, I'm Trooper Bailey with the Marlinton Police Detachment." He mentioned my father's name and wanted to know if I knew him.

"Yes. He's my father."

"Well, ma'am, I'm sorry to have to tell you, but your father was killed in a vehicle accident yesterday on Sharp's Knob."

I was stunned.

Then the officer was speaking again. He told me it appeared Dad had gotten too close to the edge of the road and it gave way, plunging Dad and his truck seventy-five feet straight down. It rolled one-and-a-half times, coming to rest on its side against a tree. He had not been found until the next day. He actually died on October 16.

"As near as we can tell, he died from the injuries in the accident, ma'am. The medical examiner will be calling you shortly."

All I said was "Oh, no." I burst into tears. What he was telling me didn't seem real. As if from a great distance, I heard the trooper say he had Dad's wallet, with eighty-one dollars inside, and a twenty-two rifle under lock and key at the Marlinton State Police Detachment in Pocahontas County. The truck had been towed, however, to Cowen, in Webster County, an hour away from the site of the accident. The remainder of his effects were in the truck.

"Did your father drink, ma'am?" The policeman was speaking to me again.

"Drink? Well, I guess so . . . umm, from time to time. Why?"

"Well, we smelled whiskey on him, and there was an open bottle of whiskey in the truck cab."

I didn't know what to say.

A half-hour later, the medical examiner called. She told me the actual cause of death was head trauma. She said, "He's also got a bruise on the left side of the neck and bruising on his back. I think he has a broken pelvis, too. Sweetheart, did he drink?"

"Drink? Yes, I suppose so. I mean, yes, binge drinking from time to time."

"Well, the trooper told me he smelled alcohol on your father. He also found a bottle of whiskey."

I glanced at my husband. He frowned and mouthed, "What's wrong?" I shook my head. "Yes, he told me."

"How long had he been drinking? I mean, last few years . . . ?"

I hesitated, not sure what to say. "All his life. Since he was thirteen. But . . . I don't know if he was drinking. It'd been over a week since I'd spoken with him . . ."

"Well, honey, I think he died instantly from the head trauma," she repeated. "I don't think he suffered."

"Um, that's good. I mean, I'm glad he didn't suffer."

"Are you the only child?"

"Yes." *What did that mean?*

"I found a photo in his wallet of a beautiful young lady. Is that you?"

"Oh, no. Not me. It's my daughter. His only grandchild."

"She's lovely. He must have been proud of her."

"He was."

# CHAPTER 36

# ATTENTION K-MART SHOPPERS! DO THE DEAD WEAR UNDERWEAR?

My father's funeral was scheduled on October 20 when I realized I had no clothes for him. I decided to dash out to K-Mart. He wouldn't have had anything suitable with him on the mountain, and in any case, I couldn't get his effects from down south in time for the funeral. I turned to my husband. "He definitely wasn't a tie kind of guy, so that's out. This should do," I was looking at the clothes in my hand—a dark grey checked shirt and black Dockers-like pants. "Um. What about underwear? Do you think I should take any to the funeral home? I mean, do they put underwear on people? And socks? What about shoes?"

My husband, digging through the belts, after realizing my dad would need one of those, started tiptoeing as if on hot ground. "Where he might be going, ooh, ouch, he'll need shoes!" I smacked him a good one on his arm.

"Well, get serious. Should I bring underwear? How about those Fruit of the Loom tighty whities you don't like and never wore?"

"Sorry. Um, sure. He can have a pair of those and a pair of my socks. Shoes?"

"No. I can't buy him shoes. He wore an 8EEE. I'd never find those anywhere. You can't see a person's feet anyway."

Later that day, we took the clothes to the funeral home. I handed them to the funeral director. "I brought underwear. I wasn't sure about that . . ."

"Oh, we put everything on them just as if they were here."

"Well, okay. I just thought you should arrive on the other side, wherever that is, looking good to go. I guess . . . he wasn't a tie-wearer, so I didn't bring one."

"That's fine. Whatever you'd like."

"I didn't bring shoes. He wears an odd size."

"Oh, that's always optional, but we do what the people like. Sometimes, people have big feet and we can't get the casket closed, so we have to remove their shoes." He made a shoving down motion with his hands. "Some people have clown feet, like mine." I dared not look at my husband. I hid a giggle behind a cough.

"Come into my office, and we'll discuss the final preparations."

We followed him into the same office I'd been in just three years earlier for my mother's funeral. We sat opposite Luke, the young funeral director.

"Well, I was afraid there'd be a problem with your dad, but it turned out fine."

"What do you mean?"

"When I talked to the funeral home director in Pocahontas County, I asked him if he would embalm your father because it had been at least twelve hours since he'd died." I looked puzzled, I'm sure. He explained.

"A human decays ten times faster than any animal on the planet. It's all that junk food we consume."

"Oh."

"The funeral director over in Marlinton didn't seem to want to take care of your father, so when we got him here last night, I was afraid we'd run into problems."

"I don't follow."

"The funeral director told me the medical examiner had tried to get blood from his femur and couldn't do it."

I'm sure I looked blank.

"That means probably internal injuries. The blood would have bled out of his veins and clotted."

"Oh."

Luke was leaning over his desk. He looked prepared to launch into further explanation.

"But you were successful with my father. I mean, no problems, right?"

"No. No problem. It . . . he turned out fine."

"Oh, good." We briefly discussed payment for the funeral, then made movements to leave.

"I noticed they're bulldozing next door," I said.

"Yeah! Ain't that a big pile of dirt? It's going to be for additional parking. I've been out all day watching them. Had to have them move the same dirt three times!" Now, he was leaning forward, animated.

"Uh, well, if there's no more to discuss, I'll be going now. I have family at home. We'll be back tonight, one hour before the viewing."

"We'll see you then."

"Thanks."

We walked out of the funeral home. I said to my husband, "That was more information than I needed. And it's clear that young Luke is missing his calling. Digging things up is more along his line, rather than burying."

At home, I brewed a pot of coffee and considered the clothes I'd bought for my father's funeral. I was fortunate that with my mother, my aunt had gathered the outfit Mom wanted to be buried in. Although I'd gotten the wrong wig, everything else seemed in place.

I carried my cup of coffee outside to our deck. The air was cool and the sky overcast. Leaves were changing, and nature seemed to be promising a damp fall. Sipping the hot liquid, I considered what went unsaid between my mother, father, and me. Many of us never finish conversations, and then when we have no more chances, we live with regret.

Sitting in a swing, looking beyond my backyard, I considered the space between the trees and the sky. How big was that space, really? Miles? Or only a few feet, as the optical illusion seemed to be telling me? No heat wavered the air; no blue sky for me to wonder why it was blue. Only mist, grey like my mother's eyes. All an illusion of the distance between my father and me.

# CHAPTER 37

# WE SHALL GATHER

At the viewing on Sunday night, I met Dad's oldest and dearest friend, Zeph Christian. Although I'd heard about Zeph all my life, I'd never been to the mountains to meet him. Dad had hunted and fished with Zeph for decades and spoke of him and his family often. He came toward me, leaning heavily on a cane, steadied by a woman near my age who had her hand through the crook of his arm. He introduced himself and his daughter, Jane.

"Aye, God, I can't believe it," he said, nodding toward Dad in his casket.

"I know, Zeph. I just assumed he'd be here another ten or fifteen years."

"We've known each other for years, me and Vernon. We go way back."

"Yes, he spoke of you often. It's good to finally meet you, but I wish it weren't like this."

****

At the funeral the next morning, the same pastor who held my mother's service was to speak at my father's. I hadn't known anyone else to call. He had interviewed me the night before for information about my dad.

"We all know Vernon lived a full life," the pastor said after the opening prayer. I dared not glance around at my relatives who had gathered to say good-bye to my father. If I had, I'm sure in the midst of grief and sadness, we would have had to stifle giggles. "A full life" was the understatement of the century. He had said he didn't know my father, but I began to wonder what the heck I'd told him.

My father was to be interred in the mausoleum with my mother. When we arrived, my head felt built of lead as I reluctantly looked up at the gaping hole where my mother's casket was, fortunately, out of view. The black hole in the wall seemed cold, sinister. I glanced back over my shoulder and took in the scene. It was remarkably similar to the one I viewed at Mom's funeral three years and two weeks earlier. The leaves were turning to glorious colors. The sky was a clear blue. A gentle breeze eased around us as we stood up on the hill overlooking the cemetery. It was quiet, with only the occasional cry of geese honking their way south.

\*\*\*\*

When I called the Marlinton Police Department after the funeral to see when I could pick up my father's effects, the sergeant on duty told me it would be a few days before they would let me come for them. They were short-staffed, and only one person had the key. I told him what I hadn't told Trooper Bailey earlier: "Sergeant, my father had in excess of fifteen hundred dollars on him and possibly a checkbook. Trooper Bailey indicated all he had of value of my father's was eighty-one dollars and a gun. My dad never carried all of his money in his wallet at one time, preferring to hide it in his luggage or in the truck. Did items fall out of the truck?"

He said, "Yes, ma'am, they did. But we put them back in the truck. We found his wallet in the glove box and took the gun. We didn't see anything else that looked like a checkbook or cash, nothing else of real value."

Finally, I was cleared to pick up Dad's effects from the state police and then drive to the impoundment where they had his truck. I felt as if my father's things were scattered to the four winds, and I needed to gather, at times almost feeling feverish with impatience, frustrated I had to wait. I wanted to know what had happened.

On the way, I stopped by the Bureau of Statistics to pick up my father's death certificate. Written by a recorder who might have been left-handed, it said the immediate cause of death was "Multiple Trama [sic] due to Motor Vehicle Accident." There was no autopsy.

"Why wouldn't they do an autopsy? I thought the law was that anyone who dies without witnesses had to have an autopsy," I said to my husband as we drove to Marlinton.

"I thought so too. What else does the death certificate say?"

"Just the precise place where he wrecked, plus other personal info, date of birth, his parents, stuff like that. 'Forest Service Road 135 @ 4.6 miles South of Mine Road Sate Secondary 219/1 N. Marlinton, W.V.'" We continued to drive in silence, and I studied the death certificate as if it would tell me what happened.

"Are you going to go to the crash site?" my husband asked.

I couldn't think that far ahead. "I don't know."

After a two-hour drive, we arrived at the state police detachment to retrieve Dad's gun and wallet. Then we drove to the wrecker service that towed Dad's truck. It turned out my father's truck was taken to the wrecker driver's house. The driver, we were told, was Zeph Christian's nephew. When we got to his house, he explained, "Normally, wrecks are towed to a public wrecking yard where they would be unsecured. I volunteered to bring your dad's truck to my house and keep it here until someone came to get the items from it. I didn't know your name or the name of your daughter, his granddaughter. He just said, 'the daughter,' or 'the granddaughter,' whenever he referred to you two. That's the way we fathers are. Up here in the mountains, anyway." I said I understood.

I told him about the money and checkbook. He expressed his disgust with thieves and liars and talked about how people are raised by the old standards up here in the mountains. He had unloaded the camping gear from the back of my dad's truck, boxed and bagged all of it because fuel from the camp stove had leaked all over everything. We loaded our truck with the banged-up, broken, fuel-soaked camping gear. Two small suitcases and a shaving kit. I went through them. No money or checkbook.

I had worried about the checkbook, so I called both banks he banked with and asked them to put a hold on his accounts until I found out what he had had on him. I didn't want to head to South Carolina until I had his belongings in my possession.

As we drove out in a field to Dad's truck, I noted hound dogs, four of them, chained to small doghouses, lining the dirt track that led to the field. I counted them off by breed: a blue tick, a red tick, one all black, and a Walker hound. How would I even know if I hadn't been my father's daughter? They bayed and pulled at their chains, their silky coats gleaming in the sun.

The sky, unlike the usual milky expanse that is common in West Virginia, was a vivid, clear blue, with a few wisps of cirrus clouds. Must be a high rather than a low weather pressure over the state. I hadn't checked the weather reports. A breeze, fairly stiff, was blowing, tossing my hair in my face as soon as I got out of our truck. It was time to pay attention, to look.

My husband bolted out of our truck and over to Dad's. He turned to look back at me as I stepped forward. I stopped, trying to absorb the scene before me. I said, "There's no blood, is there?" He nodded. "No. None." I came closer.

The truck didn't look as bad as I thought it would. The cab was intact, the roof crushed slightly, the hood jammed in an upward V shape. The back end of the truck was crushed pretty badly, though. A gaping hole in one side of the topper indicated where a tree limb had gone through. I wandered around and around it. Just looking but not really thinking. I noticed the keys still in the ignition and another set hanging on the doorknob. Someone had found them and hung them. I said to my husband, "You know, if they found these keys and returned them to the truck, why didn't they find money or a checkbook?" He didn't answer.

The next day, I made the trip to my Dad's home in South Carolina. The state of West Virginia told me I had to go south to begin probating his will, and I had to act fast because I couldn't find anything out about his checking accounts until I had papers saying I was legally entitled to do so.

I walked in his house—the extra keys in his truck turned out to be house keys—and sensed immediately the house was waiting for my father. His work shoes sat beside his chair, a *Globe* magazine lay open to his crossword puzzle, his coffee cup sat in the sink. Later in the evening, I changed into pajamas and sat in my mother's chair, picked up the *Globe* magazine, and tried to finish my father's crossword puzzle.

The answers eluded me.

# CHAPTER 38

# RIDING ON COMETS

It was late on one of my school nights, 1:30 a.m., when my father knocked on my bedroom door. "Get up, Cat," he called. "Come out on the porch."

I stumbled out of bed and outside. It was February. My pajamas provided no protection from the freezing temperature. My father stood at the edge of the porch. I knew he'd just gotten home from the evening shift. He pointed to the sky. "Look," he said.

Poised against the black sky was a perfect-shaped comet. "It's Bennett's Comet. It seems as if it's standing still, but it's moving thousands of miles an hour," he told me. I forgot I was chilled or how long we stood gazing. I heard him add, "Ain't that something."

My father quit school after the tenth grade to go to work for food and clothes. He continued to learn all his life. *National Geographic* was one of his favorite magazines. We walked the woods identifying trees, plants, bugs, and even snakes. He loved the sky. I recall the day he pointed out Sirius, the Dog Star. "It's dog days now," he warned. "Wounds won't heal." He told me a ring around the moon meant rain was coming. We found the North Star, the Big Dipper. Identified Mars and Venus.

My father gave me the gift of curiosity, and my mother gave me the gift of being grounded. Her circumstances meant she, too, dropped out of school to work for food and clothes. Through her struggle with depression, she taught me what it means to endure the adversities of life. An avid reader, she led me to love books and writing.

When I graduated from high school, my father said he would attend. When the day came, he wasn't there. "He's working overtime," Mom said. She wouldn't attend either. When I was older, I realized the truth: neither thought they had appropriate clothes, and perhaps they felt uncomfortable with how to behave in a public situation they had never experienced. When I stepped from the stage after receiving my diploma, I turned to face classmates, other parents, and teachers, but no face that resembled mine.

At the graduation party, I stepped away from the bonfire my classmates had built in a vast field and studied the night sky. The Milky Way shimmered like a stone path to the immense universe. I was hurt neither parent had attended my graduation. Yet, I realized no schoolteachers had taught me to love learning as my parents had. My parents never said it exactly, but I knew from many conversations: I could be whoever I wanted to be. At that moment, I chose not to be bitter. Over time, the hurt eased, and I realized that though my parents were earthbound, they wanted me to ride on comets, lifted skyward from their humble shoulders.

# CHAPTER 39

# NIGHT ON CHEAT MOUNTAIN, PART 3

On top of Gauley Mountain in eastern West Virginia, a trickle of water streams downward and rapidly—in no time at all it seems—it becomes the Gauley River. The trout-filled stream grows wider, then flows from the base of the mountain until it joins with the New to form the Kanawha, which rushes to the Ohio, and thus strengthened, surges on to the Mississippi and beyond.

The genesis of rivers seems to be in wild places, and from the top of Gauley, within the embrace of thousands of trees covering mountains; we hear the howling of the coyote, feel the velvet flap of an owl's wing as it nearly misses your head as it soars, looking for its next meal. If you're lucky, you might spot one of the fabled mountain lions. The forest rangers say no such things exist, extinct from the area long ago, but natives and the occasional visitor will tell of seeing a tawny cat, with a tail as long as its body, watching from the edge of the woods. Once, the phantom animal disappears into the dark of the forest, we have a good yarn to tell. Listeners might scoff, but hairs standing up on the back of your neck don't lie. These wild places spawn stories. Stories that flow down into the valleys to become family legends.

On a warm November day, I stood on top of Gauley Mountain

looking down an embankment where my father had rolled his truck to his death. The elderly man at my side, eighty-three-year-old Zeph, pointed to smudges in the mud down a hillside. "See that?" he asked me and pointed to a faint impression in the mud. "That there is where a bear went down the hillside. And see over there? That there is where another one, a mite smaller, went up. I wonder what they wanted?"

I nodded, not really seeing any tracks at all, but I wasn't about to be contrary to an old mountain man. He and my father had hunted bear and deer for decades, running the mountains like old warriors. They knew little fear due to their intimate knowledge of the land. Now, on top of Gauley, I stood by the old man's side and wondered what he must feel at losing an old friend. Did he care? How much? What did I know about him, and how he felt? Nothing. I instinctively knew not to ask. You don't ask mountain men how they feel. I knew he'd known tragedy aplenty. He'd lost his wife to cancer a few years earlier, and he'd lost his son, daughter-in-law, and grandson to a freak lightning strike beside Smith Mountain Lake in Virginia. A storm had brewed, and for safety, they brought their boat in off the water and were standing beside the lake as the storm approached. Lightning hit a tree next to them, traveled down through the tree and into the roots on which they were standing. It killed them all instantly. How do you reconcile losing so many in your family at once, let alone to a random and bizarre lightning strike?

Zeph raised his head at a sudden cool breeze. "Feel that?" I nodded as I rubbed my bare arms. "That means rain's a-comin,'" he said as he turned and made his way back to the car. He was done talking.

Nearly fifty years after the raucous night on Cheat Mountain with his father, my father was on top of Gauley Mountain driving his pickup along Sharp's Knob. The pull of mountains and the rivers had remained strong in him, even after he'd retired and moved to South Carolina.

The land in that part of West Virginia was as sacred to my father as anything. A religion, almost, and a feeling and belief it was where he always wanted to be. In the mountains, he communed with animals and trees and listened to whatever gods it was that told him it was okay to drink himself nearly into oblivion.

No one knows what happened for sure. He'd told a nearby camper he was going to take a drive. The other man, an avid fisherman of the elusive brown trout, and who'd only met my father once before, told him, "Okay, Vernon. I'll have a good mess of fish cooked up for this evening." My Dad laughed, so the man told me later, and that's the last time anyone saw him alive.

The road on top of Gauley Mountain is not paved, but its gravel is beaten down well. When the road my father drove along—a forest service road—curved, my Dad's truck did not. The road did not give way, as the policeman had speculated. My Dad, for whatever reason, didn't turn the wheels.

When Dad and his truck rolled down the hill, the truck came to a rest against small trees. The next day, a logging trucker, high in his rig, drove by and saw my Dad's truck lying on its side, against scraggly hemlocks. He stopped, made his way down to the truck and unable to get a door open, smashed the windshield with his axe. He reached in. My father's hand was cold.

I noticed the cool breeze had died down. The rain Zeph predicted was on the horizon. I looked in the direction of Cheat Mountain, and it rose like a specter in the darkening sky. In my mind, the revving engines faded, along with the sharp smell of whiskey. As I left, two men, speeding side by side down Cheat Mountain, roared away into the dark.

# CHAPTER 40

# FALL

In autumn, when I was a child, it rained often, making the leaf-mold smell sharpen, along with the pungent sweetness of the rich, black earth. On my way to school, I passed beneath ancient oaks. I stumbled over sturdy roots of spent fruit trees. Sweet apples fell to the ground to hungry yellow jackets that swarmed, eating their fill.

If it was dry, the dusty leaf mold coated the inside of my nose. Lethargy moved like an odorless gas through sun-warmed rooms at school. Dressed in brown corduroy pants and a turtle-neck sweater, I drowsed in the heat with my classmates. I struggled to concentrate as I watched the season transform the view outside our windows.

One October morning, when I was ten, I discovered my mom out in the backyard hanging our washed clothes. Clear sky, grass shiny with dew, crimson leaves lay scattered under a maple. When they dried later in the day, I remembered thinking, I'll rake the leaves into a pile and jump in them.

Mom's hands were cracked and red from the cool air and cold, wet sheets as she methodically pegged them on the line. Around the corner of the house came Dad, returned from an early squirrel hunt, his shotgun broken down, hanging over his arm, his blaze orange hat askew. In one hand were two fox squirrels—his catch as the sun rose. He approached my mother, and wiggled the dead squirrels in her face and teased her about eating squirrel brains with her scrambled eggs. She pushed him away with her free hand. I remember their laughter as I swirled among the brilliant white sheets.

Dad skinned the squirrels, and Mom fried them for supper. I wouldn't eat any of it, but I marveled at the tiny bones in the trash. Later, I jumped and rolled in the leaves until I had thumped my tailbone on the hard ground one time too many. I rustled through the leaves and made my way to the house and to bed. Mom checked on me, to see if I'd brushed my teeth. My Dad commented on my leaf-piling and jumping abilities. Then later I lay listening to the sound of my parents' gentle snoring, hearing their laughter in my mind as I drifted to sleep.

How could I have known then they would both die in October forty years later, and I'd walk the path to their graves under a clear blue sky, with fallen leaves, edges curled, crunching under my feet.

Did I say to the gathered bereaved that my world had felt safe because of my parents? I know they would have wondered, but it is what I felt most of the time?

As a child we think those golden moments and our parents will last forever. But lives, like leaves on maple trees, fall after a time, to lie waiting for someone to gather the memories of them, to feel joyous once more under a weakening sun.

STRENGTH . . .

# CHAPTER 41

# LIMINAL

ON A CRISP, PREDAWN MORNING, my fifty-fifth birthday—October 31—unable to sleep, I stepped out onto my deck into a preternatural silence. The sky shimmered with stars in numbers I rarely get to see in our light-polluted suburban valley.

Resisting the chill, I rubbed my arms and twirled slowly, staring up. I wished I were more versed in recognizing the sky's constellations rather than just the Big Dipper and Orion's Belt,—the few Dad had taught me—but all I saw as I spun like the Earth were more scattered stars, forming no patterns.

Then I focused my vision to the north, but as I turned my head, I glimpsed from my peripheral vision a large shape in the sky—a fuzzy, green ball. I turned my head to stare directly at it, but it refused to become clear. I slid my line of sight slightly to either side, and it still eluded me as to what it was. A galaxy? A nebula? A spaceship? I had no idea, but I knew it was unusual.

Two days later, I read that the green ball was the Comet Holmes, which had exploded, creating a massive green coma around it from the debris. No history of the comet mentioned—just the fuzzy orb in the night sky that would remain for another week or so then fade.

A few months later, I joined a local astronomy club, determined to learn constellations and deep-space objects. From a speaker's lecture, I learned Comet Holmes had not exploded; rather, in its travel past Jupiter, the planet's gravity had pulled bits of the comet from its core. The debris heated, sparking the coma we'd all seen—a massive round cocoon that grew to be the largest object in our solar system. Larger than Jupiter or the sun.

It turns out Comet Holmes had passed our way and created this same light show 120 years ago. We apparently had forgotten it because it caught everyone off guard when it passed this way again. When it returns in 2127, perhaps it won't survive the pull of Jupiter and will explode for real. We can only wonder what spectacle it might present to our great-grandchildren.

Looking up at the sky made me feel a part of the grander scheme of things, but my core, my middle remained wobbly and unsure. I struggled to be without all those giants in my life who had passed on.

I began to understand I was like Comet Holmes. With their deaths, bits and pieces of me seemed blown away, losing critical mass. After years of living with my past, my grandparents' and parents' legacies, their stories, I realized I had not built a story of my own. In a way, I was still a little girl watching giants fight.

****

I had lived a long time in my head and in the past. One warm spring day, I felt the urge to get in my car and drive, frustrated with thinking about writing my own story. The day seemed soft and unformed. Motes of pollen drifted in the rays of the sun. The pollen burdened my body so that I resisted movement; it blurred the path to clear thought and clarity of purpose. That is what I thought as I tied my tennis shoes, then found my car keys and left the house. Not a good omen to clear my head of the past and to think about my future.

After I drove for a few minutes, I popped in my favorite CD, called "Mom's Mix," made by my daughter, who downloaded my favorite songs. I drove down Route 60, which runs parallel with the interstate. When Route 60 was cut, it followed the old James River Turnpike, a road that respected hills and farms, unlike the interstate, which bullied its way through the countryside as if being straight as an arrow was all we were to think about. Then suddenly I was at my family's cemetery.

It is orderly like most large cemeteries, urging you to go one way and not the other, so that cars meeting won't have to venture off onto the grass and create tracks to mar the perfection. It wasn't so long ago that folks buried their own on near ground, family cemeteries that through the decades became neglected and overgrown with a real sense those goodly people would return to dust, and then begin a proper forgetting as the decades flew by.

A friend once lamented, "I wish I had my own cemetery." We had been discussing a poem in which the poet describes her 150-year-old family cemetery. It is land they can claim in a most definite way. No one will sell their cemetery or move their bodies because no minerals lie underneath. The bodies will remain until the earth stops spinning. It was this permanency my friend was lamenting. This laying claim to land that is layered not only with family bodies but family memories.

Different sections of the cemetery I had just turned in to had flat bronze plaques or granite tombstones. A few graves had small lights around them that glow eerily at night as if the wandering dead need to be shown the way back.

My car glided up the hill, motor hum barely disturbing the quiet, to the mausoleum, where my parents are. I parked the car on an incline, hoping my emergency brake held. I slipped around to the east side of the square, granite building, passing the front windows, where inside are comfortable wing chairs for the bereaved. I stepped around the corner and turned to squint at my parents' plaque ten feet up. The name Hodges is etched in copper, surrounded by dogwood blossoms in relief.

I didn't linger long but wished I'd brought a step-ladder and flowers. I left pondering: Where are my parents, really? On a shelf, ten feet up? I did not think so.

One night, my answer came in a dream. In the dream, the dead and the living walked the same ground but did not seem to see one another. I saw my grandmother stride by, dead by this point for thirteen years. I saw my aunt, who was alive, walking by as well. No one seemed to see me. Then my mother appeared and strode in my direction, carrying a shopping bag. Her head turned, and she saw me. I ran to her and hugged her. "I love you, Mom." I said. I stood back a bit to actually see her so near to me.

She was happy. Her cheeks rosy, her blonde hair perfectly coiffed, always a concern to her in life—"How's my hair?" she always asked as soon as I came for a visit. White capris and blouse, vivid jacket of blues, greens, and golds. "This is Heaven," she told me. "I get to go to yard sales all day long, and the bargains are everlasting."

She pointed to a nearby hill. On top of the hill stood my father. She said, "You should go to him. You need to see him."

I turned and walked toward him and saw no one passed near him. He stood, head down, incredibly sad-looking. The closer I got, the more I felt physically weighed down. It was loneliness. Overwhelming loneliness. I knew that was what he was feeling. I also knew in that moment he would be alone, with no one and nothing in his space, to speak to him, to acknowledge him, for a long, long time. I clutched my chest at the pain of his sorrow. Eventually, I realized, he would come out of the bubble of loneliness and join others, but it would be a long haul, in time humans can't calculate.

When I was four, and I watched my great-grandmother in that white light, I asked the adults what was wrong with her. She's dying, they said. Later, I wondered where heaven was. What did it mean to die? What was heaven? Questions from decades ago. Perhaps I did not know the answers for sure, but it gave me comfort to have seen my parents, where they are. It gave me hope my father would be forgiven. I knew forgiveness had to begin with me.

# CHAPTER 42

# DRAGON'S TALE

I SIT ON SOGGY GROUND, and around me is evidence of recent snow. Beside me is a downed pine tree with only a few needles clinging to the limbs. I stroke the winter-beaten grass between frigid fingers. I remember seeing an aerial photograph of this small farm where I am now, which once belonged to my grandparents. The photo reveals the land's shape. Fronting the hollow road, a broad yard gradually tapers to a narrow field, so slender it seems to writhe between the hills. The end of the field, where I am, is arrow-shaped. My uncle, who now lives in my grandparents' house said, "You know, it looks like a dragon's tail."

I can't see that shape from where I'm sitting, but I know I am at the very pointed tip of the arrow. Behind me hills rise to form a ridge, over which is another family's property. All around me turtle-shaped hills rise, their backs covered with hard-woods. Near me, a spring I call Persephone burbles from underground and flows toward the creek. Persephone's path stains the grass like tears on a cheek. Someone once buried a culvert in the spring's path, but it is broken, and water runs around it.

The cold convinces me to leave this narrow tip of land and

return to the warmth of my grandparents' home place. I am grateful I can come back.

Trundling over a small hillock, I remember back in the 1980s, loggers cut selected trees and dragged them away. Thirty years later, the remaining trees have thickened their girth and deepened their roots as if lending stability and strength to the soil. They are red oak and black oak, red maple, and hickory. Nearer the creek are walnut and sycamore. As I walk, the ground feels spongy on the surface, but it's as if something tensile lies underneath the dull grass and moldy leaves; I imagine it is a dragon's tail coiled, at peace at last.

I crest another knoll and stop to admire the small, white bungalow; it looks so peaceful softening in the late winter sun.

****

This was my father's childhood home, his world, and all through my childhood we lived here on and off and visited often. Though my parents and I moved around, from rental to rental, my grandparents' farm is the place I think of when I think of home. It was the one constant place I knew until I was grown and married with a home of my own.

This land helped shape my father and those before him. Each generation has responded to the land, what it offered, in different ways. I keep returning, not just to remember my family or what it is this land has always meant to me; I want to know how this land shaped me, too.

****

This place first supported agrarian then working-class people. My great-great-grandfather raised tobacco and timber on the larger parcel of land granted by Governor Wise of Virginia in 1863, just a few months prior to West Virginia forming from the strife of the Civil War. Another great-great-grandfather built a log home in 1870, just up the hollow. He farmed and timbered. His son, my great-grandfather, grew up in the log home and became a schoolteacher and farmer. His son, my grandfather, the one who had this home built, became an expert welder at a local gas company. His son, my father, worked in the rolling mill section at an aluminum plant a couple hours away.

The land, to these men, possessed a practicality, a way of living for all families down through time. If the land's beauty or wildness spoke to them, they never mentioned it. Small creatures—rabbit, squirrel, and larger ones such as turkey and deer—were supported by the land, which in turn supported family. The men hunted and fished, tilled gardens, and cut trees for lumber to build homes, outbuildings, furniture. A clearing, which revealed the shape of a dragon's tail, was formed purely by accident. The clearing was where they pastured cattle, planted gardens, or built barns, corn-cribs, and pig-pens, not mowed to be fanciful shapes.

Only the corn-crib remains. All other outbuildings have been torn down, no longer needed. I pass the crib as I continue my walk toward the house. It houses a tractor used to mow the yard and field. I slow when I hear the high-pitched *screeeeee* of a red-shouldered hawk. I watch him ride thermals over my head, hunting for mice or voles brave enough to come from underground and forage for seeds or the half-frozen bug or worm. The sky is milky. West Virginia's millions of acres of trees create humidity that softens blue skies. Breathing in deeply, I close my eyes and imagine the dragon under the soil, rolling over in its eternal slumber. His stirrings flip up images and sounds from long ago . . .

****

As the hawk's call dies away, a strong image comes to me: at the edge of the backyard, over by the creek, my father, his brothers, and cousins work on car engines, then race their vehicles up and down the dirt road, puffing out dust coating everything. They cut the engines, but the quiet does not last long. The men swagger about, beers in hand. They brag about which type of engine is superior, and a lack of agreement leads them to fist-fights.

It is still light, moving on toward evening. The brawl continues, but I am absorbed in catching minnows in a chipped coffee cup. My father and an uncle move toward one another, then fall to the ground, rolling over and over, grunting. The other men hoot and holler, encouraging the fight. Too late, I notice them roll near me. The ground seems to quake as one man rises, then is slammed to the ground in a shoulder pin. My minnows forgotten, I flee up the hill toward deep woods.

Reaching the hill's height, I notice in the dimming light the moss underfoot softens my footfalls. I stop. The silence is profound, save my gasping breath. A rotting log provides a seat, and I sit in the stillness until my heart stops trying to come out of my chest. I am protected by tall trees and large boulders. Small beetles scurry over leaf litter and lichens. No birds sing—it is too late in the day. I breathe in primal air. It stills me. The woods allow me to stay until I know the earth has stopped quaking in my grandmother's backyard. Only then do I return.

****

At this moment, as I am standing in the chilling air, the memory of fleeing to a lovely, benign forest fades from my mind. In its place, another memory rises. On the opposite side of the yard where my father and his brothers fought, my grandmother emerges from the cellar, carrying a large galvanized tub full of canning jars. The garden produce must be preserved. My job is to wash the jars, and then my grandmother scalds them. With sure hands, she peels fruits and vegetables, readying them for the canning bath. If I am lucky, she'll slice a green apple and feed me from the blade of her knife.

On another day, she steps into the old smokehouse to wash clothes in an ancient washer that has an exposed motor at the bottom. When I was a child, the smokehouse was no longer redolent with salted hams and curing bacon. Years later, it became the washhouse, scented with washing powder and bleach. Although I am barely tall enough at four years old to reach the top of the washing machine, she lets me feed wet, green work clothes through the wringer, which is clamped on a side of the washtub. I look up to see her warm, brown eyes crinkling at the corners as she smiles. She flashes a grin in teasing sympathy after I've accidentally run my fingers through the wringer along with my grandfather's work shirt. My fingers are not broken, but the pain is powerful. Her smile turns to a purse-lipped clucking, as she reaches toward my hand, patting it, telling me she has just the remedy. I am snubbing back tears as I follow her into the house. She folds ice cubes into a dish towel and tells me to hold it around my fingers. She returns to the washhouse. Laundry for a big family will not wait.

\*\*\*\*

I let this image fade as the thought dawns that the women were shaped by the land as well. They were the ones who cooked the kill, separated the chicken from its head, canned the garden spoils, and tried to keep the men civil. Their work was much harder and yes, they did complain, but mostly about the men. Their bustle kept me on my toes, following them around, watching. If I begged hard enough, I got to help. Occasionally, my grandmother saw to it I learned to can food, hang clothes, dust furniture, wash dishes, and iron. Mostly, I ran free in the fields and up on the hills until the women called me in to supper. I was always happy when I heard their voices. I would return to find my mother or my grandmother or an aunt standing in the pool of kitchen light falling upon the backyard. I released my fireflies and scurried into the house, to grab a plate of fried chicken, mashed potatoes, and fresh corn. When the table was crowded with the adults, I carried my plate to the TV room and turned on the television. I was soon lost in a world of *Steam Boat Bob* and *I Love Lucy* reruns.

The women seemed to be reactionary, now that I think about it. They were always in response mode: to feed, to clothe, to clean, to hold the hand of the frightened, to caress the foreheads of the dying.

****

The contrast was not so clear to me when I was a child, but as an adult, I look back to the times when I sat with my family on hot summer evenings and everyone relaxed with one another—we were family then, or at least what I thought a family should be. Familiarity, laughter, storytelling—this happy trio of qualities assured me of a night of safety and comfort. After dinner, everyone left the hot kitchen for the cool of the front porch. Above us the brilliant Milky Way charted a path to the universe, and the trees on the hills came alive with firefly twinkling.

The women in my life spent an inordinate amount of time enduring, but even they could not keep the land from shaking from time to time, and when the dragon rumbled, the men rattled sabers.

Their rowdiness, their actions and reactions, appeared to me larger than life. No one offered a reason for why the men and women behaved as they did. The emotion I felt most of my young life was fear, and where there is fear, anger finds no room; I was an only child, small among giants. And no one felt the need to tell a little girl the ways of giants.

****

My mind comes back to where I am, on a small hill looking down on the little white house where so much of life happened. It is odd to think land with such a potential for violence also challenged me. Maybe the dragon was testing me, helping me find my strengths. I remember the day, when I was nine or ten, I faced the challenge. One hill adjacent to my grandparents' house rises but then levels to a ridge that continues to the mouth of the hollow.

Allowed to roam as far as I wanted, I often followed the ridge for a mile and to an outcropping of boulders. On the edge of one large boulder, a nodule of rock protrudes. Everyone in the hollow called it the Devil's Seat. Much bravery was needed to scoot out onto the Devil's Seat and dangle legs on either side, to risk falling twenty-five feet below, a drop to certain death, or so my cousins and I liked to believe.

As I approached the large limestone boulder, mottled with lichen and moss, I knew I would climb out onto the Devil's Seat, driven to conquer my fear. What fear I wanted to chase away, I couldn't have said then, but now I understand what the real fear was, and though I did not shout and demand the fighting stop, the drinking stop, the tears of my mother and grandmother dry up, climbing onto the Devil's Seat was an intuitive way of abating my fear and confusion. It was the one thing I could conquer.

I sat down on the boulder, prepared to inch my way to the seat. I risked a look over the side, and it seemed as if the ground below was terribly far down, as if I were on top of a great mountain. Smaller boulders and rocks littered the hillside. They would not be comfortable to land on. Slowly, I scooted until my feet were on either side of the seat. All I needed to do was move forward a few inches. I hesitated: a low hum surrounded me. Stilling my breath, I listened. The air felt charged, tingling. Behind me, a few yards away, huge electric towers supported taut lines sloping down the ridge and through the tree canopy. It was the power lines that hummed.

I scooted forward a little more. Now, my knees were on either side of the outcropping. A few more slow wiggles, and I became fully launched onto the Seat. My feet dangled in the air. I leaned slightly to the right and peered at the ground underneath. I felt dizzy. I jerked my head up, drew in a deep breath, and listened to the hum of the lines. I looked ahead, out beyond the precipice. Then I heard my heartbeat.

The blood pumped harder in my ears; but then I allowed the sound to calm me, just as my grandmother's heartbeat had calmed me years before, when I sat on her lap and listened to her stories—all the stories of my people.

I began to swing my feet. I looked out over the trees and thought, *This is a bird's view.* The sound of my heartbeat faded as I absorbed the stillness of the forest. A deep inhale, and all I wanted to do was ebb off the Seat and back onto the broad boulder. I inched backward, slowly. Then I felt the larger boulder behind me. I had done it. I had crawled out onto the Devil's Seat in this wild place, with no witnesses other than the insects crawling on the boulder, the electric lines humming in tune with my thoughts. I felt powerful, an odd feeling for me. If the presence, the angel, or whatever it was, from that night in my bedroom comforted me, it was now my own courage empowering me.

Standing and turning to leave, I glanced down to the surface of the big boulder. Nearly hidden by lichens was a pair of initials: WH and VH. My grandfather's and father's initials. I remembered: Anyone who conquered the fear and climbed out on the Devil's Seat earned the right to carve their initials. I found a small, sharp rock and dug and scraped and dug and scraped, barely etching into the hard rock. I didn't know if my initials would remain, but I scratched CH larger than theirs. I didn't know it then, but my own story had etched itself inside me.

****

Approaching the house, I realized my stories are intricately intertwined with my family's. I need not separate their stories or their lives from mine, from who I am. Each one of us stands in relief from the other. I had carved a place for myself into this family and into the land. Together, we will remain in story, patted, shaped, a thing created that will last.

# EPILOGUE

I saw my mother once more in a dream. All around me was a pure white light—above, below, surrounding me—yet, I felt as if I stood on solid ground. This place was unending: no beginning, no end. I waited—for what I did not know. In the distance a small dot appeared. It moved toward me, smoothly, rapidly. Abruptly, a figure stopped in front of me. The creature looked fragile, petite. No hair anywhere, on head or body. But its eyes were brown, huge and luminous. Its nose was just two tiny holes and the mouth was a small, delicate slit.

This genderless form wore no clothes, and the flesh was so translucent I saw veins of blood or a liquid passing under the parchment paper skin. In front of where the pubic area would be was a pair of flesh colored wings. The wings' edges were softly scalloped, like rose petals, each one gently folded over the other. They were not completely formed.

Is this how we come to look when we've been in heaven a while? Because, of course, this soft creature was my mother.

"I am evolving," she said. I realized she was speaking—why are her eyes no longer blue?—but she did not actually speak. The mouth did not move, yet I heard—or I knew—these were words, and they were only for me.

I fell under the spell of her brown eyes, her soft voice. I felt myself lean toward her, to absorb her beauty, her strength once again. She nodded slightly, but did not reach for me.

I ached to hear her speak again, and then she did: "I will see you one more time before I can no longer appear to you. You would not understand. I look like this now because it is the closest I can come to a form you can comprehend. But where I am now, is only joy. And one day, I will evolve into pure joy."

# AUTHOR BIOGRAPHY

CAT PLESKA IS A SEVENTH-GENERATION West Virginian, a writer, editor, educator, publisher, and storyteller. She is an essayist for West Virginia Public Radio, a book reviewer for the *Charleston Gazette*, and edited the anthology *Fed from the Blade*. Pleska has been published in literary magazines and newspapers throughout the Appalachian region. She lives in Scott Depot with her husband, one dog, four cats, and with a daughter, Katie, in nearby St. Albans.

# BOOK DISCUSSION QUESTIONS

1. Cat Pleska uses the metaphor of riding on comets for her memoir's title and cover illustration. What did this signify to you as you read the book? Where else do comets come into the story?

2. Pleska opens her memoir with a scene of an imaginative little girl secure in the comfort of her family's love. Does this introduction set the stage for the chapters that follow? If so, how?

3. In the Introduction Pleska reports she struggled to keep her family's stories in the shape in which they (the family members) formed them. In your opinion, did she succeed? How?

4. Pleska makes use of the sights and smells of childhood and the language common in an everyday family's life. Did this seem realistic? What did you like best about the use of the sights and smells of her childhood?

5. The author writes about the fears of childhood: the closet hiding devils, monsters under bed, etc. Did you experience the same fears during your childhood? What were they?

6. Have any of you experienced poltergeist-type activity in your lives? What happened?

7. Throughout the memoir some folkways and superstitions are included. Did you notice any specific to Appalachia?

8. What situations in the memoir stood out as most painful? Why? Most lighthearted?

9. Pleska admires the writing of memoirists Rick Bragg (*All Over But the Shoutin'*) and Frank McCourt (*Angela's Ashes*). Does her memoir recall their work for you? If so, how?

10. How was Pleska's father's drinking explained to her? How was her mother's mental illness explained to her? Would these situations still be handled in this way in most families?

11. Pleska says some stories "get away" from the teller and are lost in time. Is this true in your experience?

12. Why do you think the author chose to tell the story "Night on Cheat Mountain" in three voices? What differences are in the stories?

13. Chapter 36 deals with funeral details. What do they reveal about the family?

14. The memoir is set mostly in a particular era of Appalachia. How do the lives of the men, women, and children differ where you come from? How do today's children cope with the problems Pleska faced?

15. Discuss the apocalyptic dream that Pleska includes. What does the imagery tell you about the author and her thinking at the time?

16. How does Pleska bring her story full circle?

17. In the epilogue, Pleska tells the reader about a dream of her mother. Does the imagery and details reflect the chapter "A Tone" when the author is a little girl relating her first memory? If so, in what ways?

18. Was this memoir similar in its construction with others that you've read? If not, how was it different?

19. Do you think this memoir has universal appeal?

20. If you could ask the author a question, what would it be?